ART MASTERS

REMBRANDT

Claudio Pescio

◆

Illustrated by
Sergio

THE OLIVER PRESS, INC.
MINNEAPOLIS

◆ HOW TO USE THIS BOOK

Produced by
Donati Giudici Associati, Firenze
Original title
*Rembrandt
e l'Olanda del XVII secolo*
Text
Claudio Pescio
Illustrations
*Sergio
Paola Holguin
Andrea Ricciardi
Thomas Trojer*
Picture research and
coordination of co-editons
Caroline Godard
Art direction
Oliviero Ciriaci
Page design
Sebastiano Ranchetti
Editing
Enza Fontana
English translation
Susan Ashley
Editor, English-language edition
De Gibbs
Cover design
Icon Productions

Original edition copyright © 1995
Donati Giudici Associati s.r.l.
Firenze, Italia

© 2008 by VoLo publisher srl,
Firenze, Italia

This edition © 2008 by
The Oliver Press, Inc.
5707 West 36th Street
Minneapolis, MN 55416
United States of America
www.oliverpress.com

Publisher Cataloging Data

Pescio, Claudio
     Rembrandt / Claudio Pescio ;
illustrated by Sergio ; [English translation,
Susan Ashley].
     p. cm. – (Art masters)
Includes bibliographical
references and index.
     Summary: With reproductions of
art masterpieces, this book examines the
life and art of Rembrandt Harmenszoon
van Rijn and focuses on the cultural
developments of the era in which
Rembrandt lived.
     ISBN 978-1-934545-02-7
     1. Rembrandt Harmenszoon
van Rijn, 1606-1669–Juvenile literature
2. Painters–Netherlands–Biography–
Juvenile literature [1. Rembrandt
Harmenszoon van Rijn, 1606-1669
2. Artists 3. Painting, Dutch]
I. Ruzzier, Sergio II. Ashley, Susan
III. Title IV. Series
     2008
     759.9492–dc22
     [B]

     ISBN 978-1-934545-02-7
     Printed in Italy

11 10 09 08   4 3 2 1

Each double-page spread is a chapter in its own right, devoted to a key theme in the life and art of Rembrandt or the artistic and cultural developments of his time. The text at the top of the left-hand page (1) introduces the theme. The text below (2) gives a chronological account of events in Rembrandt's life. The smaller text and illustrations on the spread expand on the central theme.

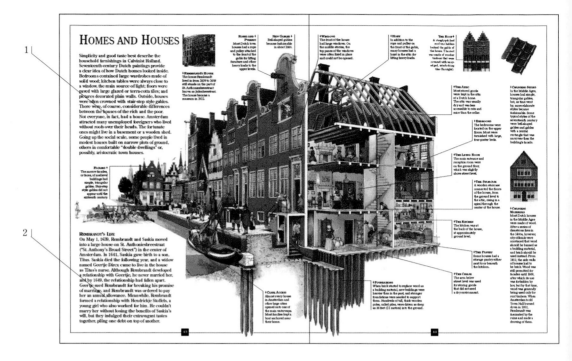

Some spreads focus on major works of art by Rembrandt. The text in the left-hand column (1) provides a description of the featured work. The text at the top of the page (2) explains the context in which the work was created, while the text below (3) offers a critical analysis of the work. The spread includes further examination of the work in the form of detailed close-ups and examples of how the work influenced other artists.

4 CONTEMPORARIES

6 FLEMISH ART

8 THE SPANISH NETHERLANDS

10 HOLLAND

12 LEIDEN

14 THE MIDDLE CLASS

16 THE BOOK TRADE

18 HISTORY PAINTING

CONTENTS

20 ANNA AND TOBIT

22 AMSTERDAM

24 PORTRAIT PAINTING

26 A PAIR OF PORTRAITS

28 LAND OF FREEDOM

30 SCIENCE AND PAINTING

32 LANDSCAPES

34 THE ANATOMY LESSON

36 FOREIGN TRADE

38 CARTOGRAPHY

40 VERMEER

42 HOMES AND HOUSES

44 GENRE PAINTINGS

46 THE REMBRANDT FAMILY

48 THE WORKSHOP

50 THE NIGHT WATCH

52 ETCHING

54 SELF-PORTRAITS

56 STILL-LIFE PAINTINGS

58 THE JEWISH BRIDE

60 REMBRANDT'S STUDENTS

62 TIME LINE, GLOSSARY AND WEB SITES

63 LIST OF WORKS INCLUDED

64 INDEX

CONTEMPORARIES

Rembrandt was a seventeenth-century Dutch artist known for his highly original style of painting. He lived in Holland during the "Golden Age," when that nation was at the peak of its economic and cultural development. Among the era's many gifted Dutch artists, including painters Frans Hals and Jan Vermeer, Rembrandt is probably the most well-known and, possibly, the most admired and celebrated. In seventeenth-century Europe, most countries had adopted a heavily ornamented style of art known as Baroque. In Holland, however, artists tended to prefer realistic representation. The world of art in this republican and Calvinist country differed from the rest of Europe in other ways, too. Unlike artists in Italy and Spain, for example, Dutch painters did not typically have patrons, such as aristocrats or high-ranking church officials. They worked mainly for wealthy professionals and middle-class merchants. The exceptions, however, included Rembrandt, who received commissions from Prince Frederick Henry of Orange.

JAN LIEVENS ✦
(1607–1674)
Born in Leiden, Lievens began his career as an artist at the same time as Rembrandt and shared a studio with Rembrandt.

SASKIA VAN UYLENBURGH ✦
(1612–1642) Rembrandt married Saskia in 1634. She was the niece of art dealer Hendrick van Uylenburgh.

PARENTS ✦
Rembrandt's father, Harmen, was a miller. In 1589, he married Cornelia van Zuytbroeck, a baker's daughter. Rembrandt was the eighth of Harmen and Cornelia's nine children and was the only one of their sons who did not become a tradesman.

✦ TITUS VAN RIJN
(1641–1668)
Titus was the only son of Rembrandt and Saskia and the father of the artist's granddaughter, Titia.

REMBRANDT ✦
(1606–1669)
Rembrandt Harmenszoon van Rijn began his career as a history painter but soon became known for portrait painting. His own appearance is well-known from his many self-portraits.

✦ CONSTANTIJN HUYGENS
(1596–1687)
A diplomat in the court of The Hague, Huygens played an important role in Rembrandt's early commissions.

✦ HENDRICKJE STOFFELS
(c. 1625–1663)
Hendrickje became Rembrandt's companion in about 1648 and gave birth to his daughter Cornelia in 1654.

FRANS HALS ✦
(c. 1580–1666)
Hals was another great seventeenth-century Dutch artist. He was best known as a portrait painter.

PRINCE FREDERICK ✦ HENRY OF ORANGE
(1584–1647)
As the stadholder, or governor, of Holland, Prince Frederick Henry was one of Rembrandt's most important patrons.

FRANS ✦ BANNING COCQ
(1605–1655)
The captain of Amsterdam's citizens militia, Cocq was the central figure in Rembrandt's most famous painting, *The Night Watch.*

✦ BARUCH SPINOZA
(1632–1677)
Philosopher Baruch Spinoza was born in Amsterdam and became one of the greatest thinkers of his time.

JAN VERMEER ✦
(1632–1675)
This Dutch artist was a generation behind Rembrandt and was known for his extraordinary interior scenes.

NICOLAES TULP ✦
(1593–1657)
Dr. Nicolaes Tulp, a renowned Dutch surgeon, was featured in Rembrandt's group portrait *The Anatomy Lesson*, representing Holland's growing professional class.

✦ PETER PAUL RUBENS
(1577–1640)
Rubens was a Flemish artist of the seventeenth century who lived and worked in the Spanish Netherlands. He was known for his Baroque-style landscapes, portraits, and history paintings.

FLEMISH ART

The art of Holland's Golden Age had its roots in a style of painting that flourished in Flanders two centuries earlier. Flemish artists were known innovators of style, subject matter, and technique. In particular, they invented, or re-invented, oil painting. They also led in developing the genres of portrait and landscape painting. The art of fifteenth-century Flanders and seventeenth-century Holland had many similarities. Both schools adopted a distinctive realistic style, taking great care to portray the smallest details. In both schools, painters responded to a demand for art from members of a wealthy, cultured middle class.

♦ PORTRAIT WITH A SELF-PORTRAIT
In the background of Jan van Eyck's double portrait *Giovanni Arnolfini and His Wife*, a mirror reflects the backs of the subjects, but it also reflects the painter, standing at the doorway of the room with another person.

REMBRANDT'S LIFE

Rembrandt Harmenszoon van Rijn lived from 1606 to 1669. At the start of his career, in the 1620s, an artist's position in society was still defined by the rules and ideas of the Middle Ages. Associations called guilds governed the activities of artists and craftsmen, just as they had in fifteenth-century Flanders. Every city had its own painters' guild. New members had to be approved by their elders, and strict rules dictated not only standards of quality but also how work was organized and what prices could be charged. Rembrandt's work helped transform the rigid guild system.

MIDDLE-CLASS ♦ SUBJECTS
Jan van Eyck (c. 1390–1441) was one of the great pioneers of fifteenth-century Flemish painting. Stories say van Eyck invented oil painting. He was also active in Flanders' political and cultural centers. Van Eyck's patrons included many rich merchants and other members of the wealthy middle classes. The couple portrayed in his painting *Giovanni Arnolfini and His Wife*, 1434 (National Gallery, London) were fabric dealers from the Italian city of Lucca.

RELIGIOUS ♦ PAINTINGS
In fifteenth-century Flanders, a taste for naturalism, or realistic representation, had spread to all parts of society. The realism so characteristic of Flemish painting was seen even in works with religious themes. In his altarpiece *St. John the Evangelist*, 1479 (Memling Museum, Bruges), Van Eyck's successor Hans Memling (c. 1435–1494) combines realism and intense spirituality.

PORTRAITS ♦
This young lady's mysterious gaze was captured by Flemish artist Petrus Christus (c. 1410–1473). The subject of the painting, which is simply called *Portrait of a Girl*, c. 1445 (Staatliche Museen, Berlin), was probably the daughter of a foreign aristocrat. In similarly styled portraits, however, Flemish painters also immortalized the features of ordinary citizens, including city officials, clergymen, merchants, and professional people.

✦ FEATURES AND DETAILS

Van Eyck's portrait *Giovanni Arnolfini and His Wife* includes features of Flemish paintings that are also typically seen in seventeenth-century Dutch paintings. Such features include the domestic setting, in an ordinary room with a natural source of light, and the accurate, detailed representation of objects from daily life. Some of the everyday objects in the painting, which include a chandelier, a pet dog, and two pairs of wooden clogs, are elements that appear to be both real and symbolic.

✦ THE PHYSICAL AND THE SPIRITUAL

The fascination of Memling's altarpiece comes from his great technical ability to capture the smallest physical details, as in the city scene behind St. John, and from the way the facial expressions of his figures convey their spirituality. Throughout his career, Memling's success seemed to rest on his skill in combining physical perfection and perceived feelings.

FANTASY AND ✦ LANDSCAPES

In the fifteenth and sixteenth centuries, elements of fantasy gradually found their way into Flemish paintings, as in this detail from *Hermit's Triptych* (right) 1510 (Doge's Palace, Venice), by Hieronymous Bosch (c. 1450–1516). At the same time, landscapes, such as *Huntsmen in the Snow* (far right) 1565 (Kunsthistorisches Museum, Vienna), by Pieter Bruegel the Elder (c. 1525–1569), came to be a genre in their own right.

THE SPANISH NETHERLANDS

♦ **HISTORY**
In the early 1500s, the area of Europe that approximately corresponds to the present-day nations of the Netherlands, Luxembourg, and Belgium was a group of provinces ruled by King Charles V, who, as the Holy Roman Emperor at that time, ruled much of Europe. In about 1556, Charles V gave the provinces of the Netherlands, along with Spain and Italy, to his son Philip II, who ruled as the King of Spain. Philip made the people he ruled pay heavy taxes. Through court actions known as the Inquisition, he also had people who tried to follow Protestant faiths or non-Christian religions imprisoned, or even killed, for going against the Catholic Church. The desire for religious freedom and independence led the provinces of the Netherlands to revolt against Spain. Seven northern provinces claimed their independence in 1581, but the war continued until 1648, when Spain finally recognized the Dutch Republic of the United Provinces. Except between 1598 and 1633, when they were ruled by Austria, the ten southern provinces continued to be ruled by Spain and were known as the Spanish Netherlands.

In the sixteenth century, the countries now known as Belgium, Luxembourg, and the Netherlands consisted of seventeen provinces ruled by Spain. After decades of rebellion, seven northern provinces claimed independence and became the United Provinces, often called "Holland." Spain reconquered the ten southern provinces, known as the Spanish Netherlands. Great differences developed between the south and the north. The government of the Spanish Netherlands was in the hands of a Spanish royal court, while Holland became a republic. The culture of the predominately Catholic south was repressive and controlling, while Protestant Holland was distinctly more tolerant. The art of the Spanish Netherlands was primarily Baroque. In Holland, the main form of artistic expression was simple, middle-class realism.

THE NETHERLANDS ♦
In 1581, the seven northern provinces of the Netherlands (shown in orange on the map to the right) declared their independence from Spain. In 1648, two more provinces, Maastricht and the Land of the Generality, joined the northern United Provinces (as shown on the map, far right).

ALBERT OF ♦ AUSTRIA
From 1598 to 1633, the Belgian court at Brussels enjoyed a period of great splendor under the leadership of Archduke Albert of Austria and his wife Isabella (below), whose portraits Rubens painted in 1613 to 1615.

ISABELLA OF SPAIN ♦
In 1598, Philip II gave his rights to the Spanish Netherlands to his daughter Isabella, who married Archduke Albert of Austria (above). As joint rulers of the southern provinces, Isabella and Albert created a long period of peace after four decades of war.

♦ **THE BELGIAN LION**
Cartographer Jodocus Hondius (1563–1612) is often credited with making this unusual map of the Netherlands and Belgium in 1611. It symbolized opposition to Spanish rule.

RUBENS AND WIFE ♦
Self-Portrait of the Artist with His Wife Isabella Brandt 1609–1610 (Alte Pinakothek, Munich), shows the refined, aristocratic art of Peter Paul Rubens.

A CATHOLIC ♦ CHURCH

Only a few decades after the northern provinces claimed independence, the cultural differences between north and south became too wide to bridge. In the Protestant north, styles of clothing and furnishings moved increasingly toward simplicity, while the Catholic south preferred lavish, highly decorative styles. Examples of these differences can be clearly seen in two paintings of church interiors (right and below). *The Miracles of St. Ignatius Loyola* (right), 1618–1619 (Kunsthistorisches Museum, Vienna), is the work of Catholic artist Peter Paul Rubens.

♦ RUBENS: THE ARTIST

The seventeenth-century artist who best represents the Catholic Spanish Netherlands is Peter Paul Rubens (1577–1640). Rubens is the prototype of a Baroque artist, capable of painting both historical and mythological scenes, as well as portraits and religious subjects. His vision as a painter was enriched by living in Italy from 1600 to 1608. In addition to painting, Rubens managed a large workshop in the city of Antwerp, in Belgium. Rubens also served as an advisor to Archduke Albert and his wife Isabella. His culture and learning made him welcome in all the courts of Europe.

♦ A PROTESTANT CHURCH

Church of St. Adolf at Assenfeld, 1649 (Rijksmuseum, Amsterdam), by Calvinist Pieter Saenredam (1597–1665), shows the simple architecture and bare walls of a Protestant church.

SELF-PORTRAIT ♦

This self-portrait, from about 1639, was one of the last paintings by Rubens. Even in old age, and almost paralyzed by a painful ailment of the joints called gout, Rubens remained a favorite artist of the Spanish king.

♦ OPPRESSION

A Military Expedition in Winter, c. 1590 (Kunsthistorisches Museum, Vienna), by Flemish painter Gillis Mostaert (c. 1534–1598), shows the harsh treatment of Protestant villagers in the south by soldiers of the Inquisition. Spanish oppression worked to benefit the Dutch Republic, however, as Protestant merchants, craftsmen, and noblemen fled north to Holland to escape persecution.

♦ RUBENS: THE IMAGE

In Rubens' self-portraits, the image conveyed is that of a confident, cultured, and wealthy man. His general manner and the details of his clothing show great self-assurance, a very different image from that of seventeenth-century artists in Protestant Holland. Rubens influenced Flemish court painter Anthony van Dyck (1599–1641), whose work includes paintings of the English monarchy.

HOLLAND

The United Provinces included the richest and most densely populated parts of the Netherlands. Thanks to a combination of favorable political, industrial, economic, and cultural factors, Holland reached a peak of wealth and power in the first half of the seventeenth century. The young nation built its world-power status on sea travel. Holland depended heavily on the sea for both military purposes and trading. An urban civilization grew up around its harbors, reclaiming its land and sending ships, voyagers, and merchandise across its waters. The sea was both Holland's greatest resource and its greatest threat.

♦ DEFINING HOLLAND
Although Holland was actually only one of the seven United Provinces, the name is commonly used to mean all of the republican provinces.

♦ SHIP REPAIR
After returning from a long voyage, every ship was given a complete overhaul. The ship had to be turned on its side so carpenters could remove barnacles and replace rotten planks, and caulkers could patch leaks with fresh coats of pitch, or tar.

PORTS ♦
Holland's harbors were vital centers of commercial activity. Docks were built at the ports by driving thick poles, called piles, into the seabed.

WATERWAYS ♦
Holland's dense network of canals provided inland waterways for transporting goods and passengers to and from the sea. Boats were specially outfitted so they could navigate in shallow inland waters as well as on the open sea.

BUILDING AT THE PORTS ♦
Rapidly expanding business and trade led to intense construction all along the Dutch coast. Buildings included silos and warehouses for storing grain and other goods and housing for the families of the growing numbers of construction and other workers employed at or near the ports.

♦ **PORT SCENE**
View of the Port of Amsterdam, 1620 (private collection), is the work of Dutch mapmaker Claes Visscher (1587–1652).

♦ **BRIDGES**
Drawbridges were common and necessary features at Dutch ports. Their ability to open and close allowed ships with tall masts to enter a harbor.

♦ **SHIPYARDS**
Using timber imported from Germany and Sweden, Dutch shipbuilding became a growing industry in the 1500s. By the 1600s, Holland was a strong competitor among European shipbuilders. The cost of building a ship in Holland was only 60 percent of the price charged in England.

♦ **WAREHOUSES**
In the seventeenth century, Holland was the grain store of Europe. Its ports were also filled with many other kinds of merchandise. Incoming goods would be kept in warehouses that were many stories high. Pulleys were used to hoist goods to the upper levels.

♦ **DREDGING**
Holland's canals and harbors needed constant dredging, or deepening, to clear out built-up silt, mud, and sand. Bucket dredges were first used in Amsterdam in the early 1600s. A bucket dredge consisted of a strong chain with buckets attached to one end. The other end of the chain was attached to a large wheel. Two workers turned the wheel, dragging the buckets along the seabed to fill them with silt.

♦ **ON THE DOCKS**
Processing products that came into the ports for reshipment to other destinations was often done on the docks. It was on the docks, for example, that loads of herring were salted and packed in barrels for reshipping.

♦ **HORSE POWER**
A bucket dredge was sometimes powered by an animal such as a horse.

LEIDEN

Like many cities in Holland, Rembrandt's home city of Leiden experienced extraordinary growth in the early decades of the seventeenth century. The population, which had dropped to twelve thousand in 1580, had increased to forty-five thousand by 1631. A good part of the increase was due to refugees, especially textile workers, who came from the Spanish Netherlands. Leiden is located where the Old Rhine and the New Rhine rivers flow together. A network of canals crosses the city, joining the two arms of the Rhine. In Rembrandt's day, huge fortifications and many windmills dominated the city, and Leiden's main industries were brewing and cheese making. Leiden was also the site of the Netherlands' first university, founded in 1575.

✦The Center of the City
The center of Leiden was on an island formed by the branches of the Rhine. Canals criss-crossed the island, on which a massive church, the Pieterskerk, is still a main feature.

✦A Post Mill
The *Wipmolen* windmill, or post mill, first appeared in the Netherlands in the fifteenth century. Its name comes from the fact that the whole structure of the windmill turns on a vertical post, or pivot, so its sails can always face into the wind.

The Struts ✦
Two heavy beams, called struts, braced the windmill against the force of the wind.

✦The Fortress
In the early seventeenth century, Leiden was a fortified city, where, within its city walls, the Rembrandt family had found protection after the Spanish invasion. Today, the canals still follow the perimeter of the city's old fortress. The Rembrandts' house and mill overlooked the Old Rhine.

THE SAILS
A typical windmill had four canvas-covered wooden sails. In high winds, some of the canvas would be taken in to reduce the speed of the rotating sails.

THE HOPPER
The miller emptied sacks of corn or grain into a bin called a hopper.

THE MACHINERY
A set of gear wheels converted the vertical rotation of the sails into the horizontal rotation of the millstones.

THE MILLSTONES
Corn or grain from the hopper was ground into granules or flour between heavy millstones that rotated against each other. The rotation speed of the stones had to be carefully controlled to keep from scorching the flour.

THE TAILPOLE
A miller turned a post mill to face the wind by pushing the structure's tailpole along on its wheel.

WINDMILL USES
The Dutch used windmills not only for milling corn and grains but also for grinding chalk and wood and operating machinery. Perhaps the most ingenious use of windmills, however, was for pumping water. Windmills were used everywhere in Holland because the country's flat landscape had no obstacles to block the wind.

THE REMBRANDT FAMILY HOME
The Rembrandt's home was a simple, brick structure close to the family mill.

REMBRANDT'S LIFE
Born in Leiden, on July 15, 1606, Rembrandt was the son of Harmen Gerritsz, who was a miller. Because it was customary in Holland for a son's name to include the name of his father, "Rembrandt" is followed by "Harmensz," short for *Harmenszoon*, which means "son of Harmen." Harmen's second name, "Gerritsz," denotes "son of Gerrit." The name "van Rijn" probably came from the Dutch name for the Rhine, the river along which generations of Rembrandt's family had owned a mill. Rembrandt's mother, Neeldgen (Cornelia) Willemsdr van Zuytbroeck, was a baker's daughter. "Willemsdr" is short for *Willemsdochter*, which means "daughter of Willem."

THE MIDDLE CLASS

In seventeenth-century Holland, aristocrats and the clergy had much less power than in other parts of Europe. The Dutch middle classes had the lion's share of control. Professionals and owners of craft workshops and trading companies formed guilds, which were corporations that held tremendous power in city government. The same people served on city councils and in the Dutch parliament, called the States General. In Holland's strong middle class, the world saw two somewhat contradictory faces. Its members had simple tastes, yet they were ambitious. They were thrifty, yet capable of excesses, such as "tulip mania." Two new institutions reflected these contradictions. Founded in 1609, the Bank of Amsterdam was a symbol of security and conservative caution. The Amsterdam stock exchange, founded in 1608, represented risk and adventure. It was a market without merchandise, where individuals and groups came together to finance business ventures by sharing the risks and the rewards.

THE NEW ✦ STATEHOUSE
Amsterdam's new statehouse, now the royal palace, was designed by Dutch painter and architect Jacob van Campen (1595–1657). The classically styled brick structure, built between 1648 and 1665, rests on a foundation of 13,659 wooden piles.

✦ THE OLD TOWN HALL
Before the 1600s, Amsterdam's town hall was a run-down medieval building that housed the offices of the mayor the sheriff, the city council, and other city officials, as well as Amsterdam's Exchange Bank.

✦ THE NEW CHURCH
A shortage of churches in the city of Amsterdam in the fourteenth century brought about the construction of the *Nieuwe Kerk*, or "New Church." Almost completely destroyed by fire in 1645, the church was rebuilt with its original Gothic architecture.

THE AMSTERDAM ✦ STOCK EXCHANGE
Built by Dutch architect and sculptor Hendrick de Keyser (1565–1621), the Amsterdam Stock Exchange was a meeting place for businessmen and merchants. Opened in 1611, it is considered the oldest exchange in the world.

✦ BERCKHEYDE
Dutch painter Job Adriaensz Berckheyde (1630–1693) was known for his city views. *The Courtyard of the Amsterdam Stock Exchange*, c. 1668, detail (Boymans, Rotterdam) shows daily dealings at the exchange.

BUILT ON WATER ✦
The Amstel River was only a few yards beneath the feet of merchants negotiating business deals on the floor of the stock exchange. The trading floor was open only two hours a day, and activities were strictly regulated.

MONEY ♦
In a place where so many business activities were based on buying and selling, money was very important. Many people in Amsterdam earned their livings from jobs in banking, stock trading, and minting coins.

♦ THE AMSTEL RIVER
Although Amsterdam is on the Amstel River, the water is too shallow for oceangoing vessels to travel on. Incoming ships have to anchor at the mouth of the river and transfer their cargo to smaller vessels, which are able to navigate the river to reach docks in the city.

♦ TULIP MANIA
From 1634 to 1637, people all over Holland, hoping to make huge profits, invested wildly in tulip bulbs. Prices went sky high, but the bubble burst, leaving thousands of people in financial ruin.

♦ THE WEIGH HOUSE
In Amsterdam's central market, known as the Dam, a public weigh house was considered essential. It was a place where goods for sale were officially weighed and measured. Before it was a weigh house, this building was part of a city gate.

♦ GUILDS
Most businesses were regulated by highly organized groups called guilds, whose members completely controlled certain occupations. One guild was responsible for load- and unloading ships. Another guild controlled all the shipping. Even beer haulers and mail carriers had guilds.

THE BOOK TRADE

Holland's Golden Age came at the same time as a general blossoming of art, literature, and science throughout Europe. Dutch publishers and booksellers had an advantage over the rest of Europe, however, because in Holland books were not censored. Spain, for example, had introduced strict censorship in the southern Netherlands, making it impossible to publish texts that strayed in any way from a strictly Catholic viewpoint. Censorship forced many European booksellers to seek refuge in Holland. In the fifty years between 1625 and 1675, the number of bookshops in Amsterdam increased from about eighty to one hundred eighty. The shops of Amsterdam, Leiden, and Utrecht stocked books and other kinds of publications in all languages, and attracted customers of all interests, from explorers to merchants. As Dutch booksellers filled orders for anyone from anywhere, all of Europe felt the benefits.

♦ WILLEM BLAEU
In seventeenth-century Holland, Willem Jansz Blaeu (1571–1638) was one of two particularly prominent printers and booksellers. Blaeu founded his business in 1599, in Amsterdam. Because he was also a cartographer, or mapmaker, he specialized in maps and globes. Known for his excellent nautical charts and atlases, Blaeu was appointed mapmaker of the Republic in 1633. He later became the official cartographer of the Dutch East India Company, which was a powerful shipping enterprise. Carried on by his sons, Blaeu's publishing business flourished for forty years.

♦ LOUIS ELZEVIER
A refugee from the Spanish Netherlands, Louis Elzevier (1540–1617) published his first book in Leiden in 1583, then, later, moved to Amsterdam. Elzevier published many authors whose works were banned elsewhere, including Descartes, Pascal, and Galileo. In 1674, Elzevier's bookshop had at least 20,000 titles in stock. The drawing above is one of the marks that distinguished works published by Elzevier.

♦ BOOKBINDING
The production of fine books led to new developments in bookbinding. Atlases, in particular, were richly bound, using parchment, leather, or velvet, interwoven with gold thread.

♦ READING VARIETY
The high level of literacy in Europe created a constant demand for reading material, which led publishers to provide a variety of books, including Bibles, political and religious pamphlets, and almanacs.

♦ MAPS AND CHARTS
The planisphere to the right (1665) and the chart of the Strait of Malacca to the left (1653) were both published and sold by Willem Jansz Blaeu.

LOW PRICES
Books in Holland were not expensive. Prices could be kept low because guild regulations were not strictly applied, royalties to authors were far from generous, and the rights of authors were often ignored when books were reprinted.

PRINTING AND SELLING
The activities of printers and booksellers were so closely related that both trades were often practiced at the same location.

MAPS AND ATLASES
Every bookshop displayed a large number of maps and atlases, most of which were produced by Willem Blaeu and Jodocus Hondius. Because the East India Company did not want certain information to be public knowledge, some of the printed maps were not as complete as they could have been.

REMBRANDT'S LIFE
Being the youngest of at least nine children, in a family that was fairly well-off, Rembrandt was not required, as his older brothers were, to learn a trade or to follow in his father's footsteps and become a miller. His parents sent him to school, hoping he would learn a profession or obtain a position in local government. In 1620, when he was only fourteen years old, Rembrandt was enrolled at the University of Leiden, probably to study theology. He was not there very long, however, partly due to religious clashes among the theology professors and partly because of his newfound enthusiasm and natural talent for drawing and painting.

HISTORY PAINTING

The genre known as history painting included political, mythological, and often religious subjects taken from the scriptures or the lives of the saints. In seventeenth-century Holland, this kind of painting was not very popular. It survived mainly because it was traditional, rather than because it was in demand. History painting was losing ground to genres that better suited the tastes of the new middle classes, who preferred portraits, landscapes, and scenes from daily life. History painting did, however, continue to be admired by aristocrats and people who were familiar with the Renaissance culture of Italy.

ALLEGORY ✦
In this detail from *Allegory on the Prosperity of Amsterdam*, Amsterdam is a maiden with the world in hand.

REMBRANDT'S LIFE

At age fifteen, Rembrandt was already showing an exceptional talent for drawing, so his father allowed him to give up his academic studies and become an apprentice to a local painter named Jacob van Swanenburgh (1571–1638). Van Swanenburgh was not a great master, but he was a good history painter, and he taught Rembrandt the techniques and popular subjects of the time. Rembrandt stayed in Van Swanenburgh's workshop from 1621 to 1624, after which he went to Amsterdam to study with a more talented master. His new teacher, Pieter Lastman (1583–1633), was also a history painter. Rembrandt stayed with him for six months, then returned to Leiden, where he set up a studio in his father's house and began to associate with Jan Lievens, another ambitious young painter.

HISTORICAL AND ✦ POLITICAL SUBJECTS
Allegorical paintings and works celebrating historical events were commissioned mainly by royal courts and public institutions.
1. Caesar van Everdingen (1617–1678), *The Glorification of the Burgomasters of Amsterdam* (Kunsthalle, Hamburg)
2. Ferdinand Bol (1616–1680), *Allegory for the Admiralty*, detail, c. 1660 (Historisch Museum, Amsterdam)
3. Gérard de Lairesse (1640–1711), *Allegory on the Prosperity of Amsterdam*, c. 1675 (Historisch Museum, Amsterdam)
4. Ferdinand Bol, *The Courage of Fabricius in the Camp of Pyrrhus*, 1650 (Historisch Museum, Amsterdam)
5. Philips Wouwerman (1619–1668), *Battle Scene*, 1650 (National Gallery, London)

RELIGIOUS SUBJECTS ✦
In tolerant, Protestant Holland, the purpose of paintings that illustrated stories from the Old and New Testaments was to educate believers. Because there was no official church patronage, private citizens usually commissioned works of this kind.
1. Pieter Lastman (1583–1633), *Deposition*, c. 1620 (Musée des Beaux-Arts, Lille)
2. Jan Lievens (1607–1674), *Pilate Washing His Hands*, 1625–1630 (Lakenhal, Leiden)
3. Pieter Lastman, *Susanna and the Elders*, detail, 1614 (Gemäldegalerie, Berlin)
4. Rembrandt, *Balaam's Ass*, 1626, (Musée Cognacq-Jay, Paris)
5. Gerbrand van den Eeckhout (1621–1674), *Christ in the Synagogue at Nazareth*, 1658 (National Gallery of Ireland, Dublin)

4

5

4

5

ANNA AND TOBIT

♦ TWO STUDIES
Rembrandt's early etchings and drawings include *Rembrandt's Mother in a Black Dress* (top) 1631 (Bibliothèque Nationale, Paris), and *Head* (above), c. 1636 (Barber Institute, Birmingham).

Once a rich man, Tobit is now blind and reduced to poverty. His wife, Anna, makes a humble living for them by spinning and weaving. One day, Anna comes home with a young goat. Tobit jumps to the conclusion that Anna has stolen the kid and begs her to return it. This story from the *Book of Tobit* is part of the Old Testament in Catholic Bibles. In *Anna and Tobit*, Rembrandt captures Anna's look of amazement after proclaiming her innocence, while Tobit asks God and his wife to forgive him.

REALISM AND LIGHT

In his first attempts at history painting, Rembrandt set two goals: to meticulously depict everyday details and to accurately reproduce the effects of light on the scene. Accomplishing both goals in the painting *Anna and Tobit*, Rembrandt enables ordinary observers to identify with Tobit's suffering and with Anna's anger at his unjust accusation.

DETAIL ♦
The wicker basket in the niche over the door is a true *tour de force*, or show of skill. This level of attention to detail is the sign of an artist who has the highest confidence in his technical ability.

♦ SETTING
A careful look at the darker parts of the scene reveals a bunch of garlic bulbs and a small cage by the window and a variety of pots, plates, and pitchers on the shelves in the background. These kinds of everyday details add to the realism of the painting.

LIGHT AND SHADOW ♦
Every detail of the painting is either highlighted or cast in a shadow, depending on its position in relation to the picture's two sources of light: the window and the fire at Tobit's feet.

♦ MODELS
Rembrandt's representation of Anna and Tobit was based not only on the Bible story but also on the many prints of religious subjects with which he was familiar. Two remarkable examples are an anonymous engraving (top left) of a work by Marten van Heemskerck (1498–1574) and another engraving (bottom left) by Jan van de Velde (1593–1641), based on a 1619 drawing by Willem Buytewech (c. 1591–1694). A comparison of Rembrandt's painting to these engravings suggests that he may have used them as models. In the first engraving, Tobit is praying, but the room is quite different from Rembrandt's setting. The second engraving shows a room similar to the one in Rembrandt's painting, but the husband and wife are actually in the process of quarreling. Rembrandt's work seems to combine elements of both.

REMBRANDT'S ♦ SIGNATURE
Rembrandt marked his early works with just his initials. In the lower left-hand corner of *Anna and Tobit* (above), the letters "RH," for Rembrandt Harmensz, are followed by the date. On later works, he started adding an "L" for *Leidensis*, which means "of Leiden." After he became famous, he simply signed "Rembrandt," possibly imitating Italian masters such as Michelangelo, Leonardo, and Raphael, who often used only their first names.

♦ A VARIATION
The story of Anna and Tobit was a part of the *Book of Tobit* typically overlooked by other painters. Rembrandt, however, went back to this story several times. In 1645, he painted the panel *Tobit Accusing Anna of Stealing the Kid*, which portrays the old man in the act of admonishing, or scolding, his innocent wife.

GERRIT DOU ♦
Born in Leiden in 1613, Gerrit Dou is believed to be Rembrandt's first student. He worked with Rembrandt during the years 1628 to 1631. What attracted him to Rembrandt was the master's skill in portraying details. Dou adopted this aspect of Rembrandt's work, along with a scrupulously natural style. In Dou's version of Anna and Tobit (*Anna and Tobit in His Blindness*, 1630, National Gallery, London), the subject and style are so similar to Rembrandt's as to suggest that the artists collaborated.

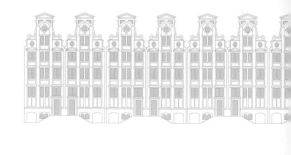

AMSTERDAM

♦ LAND AND WATER
A fair percentage of the Dutch population lives below sea level, which explains the names "Netherlands" and "Low Countries." Like much of the rest of Holland, the land on which Amsterdam stands has been reclaimed, thanks to centuries of human labor, from the waters of the North Sea. The diagram above shows how a bank of earth, called a dike, was used to hold back the water from the land.

Amsterdam's characteristic smells during the Golden Age were of tar, beer, pepper from the Molucca Islands of Indonesia, and brine for pickling herring. In its day, this city was Europe's greatest marketplace. Amsterdam grew from an average-sized town to a great metropolis in only a few decades. As new residential areas were built, the city's canals were constantly being pushed further out and its port enlarged. In 1631, French philosopher René Descartes wrote about living in Amsterdam, " . . . everybody is so intent on making a profit that I could spend my whole life here without anyone being aware of my presence." But Descartes also wrote, "In what other country could a person enjoy such complete freedom?" Before long, Amsterdam would be overtaken by London and Paris, but, for a short time, it was the wonder of the Western world.

THE AMSTEL RIVER

AWAITING ♦ DEVELOPMENT
Within Amsterdam's circle of fortifications were areas of land still to be developed.

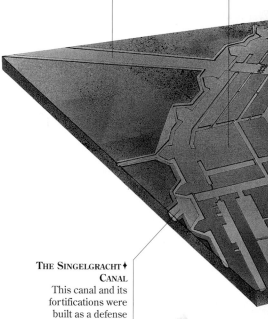

DUTCH POLDERS ♦
Polders are areas of low-lying land that have been reclaimed from the sea. Many centuries ago, much of the land that is now the western Netherlands was underwater. Between the fifteenth and seventeenth centuries, dikes were built to protect coastal areas from flooding so they could be used to grow crops.

NORTH SEA

Amsterdam

Fifteenth Century

NORTH SEA

Amsterdam

Seventeenth Century

THE SINGELGRACHT ♦ CANAL
This canal and its fortifications were built as a defense system to protect the expanding city of Amsterdam.

REMBRANDT'S LIFE
By 1628, Rembrandt had made a name for himself as a painter. He also took on his first student, Gerrit Dou (1613–1675). By 1630, the same year Rembrandt's father died, Rembrandt and Lievens had been noticed by Constantijn Huygens (1596–1687), a Dutch diplomat in the court of The Hague, which was the center of government in Holland. Huygens wrote that the two artists "are already on a par with the most famous painters and will soon excel them." In Lievens, Huygens saw great inventiveness, in Rembrandt, an extraordinary ability to represent emotion. Rembrandt soon decided to leave Leiden and venture into a wider market. In 1631, he moved to Amsterdam and met Hendrick van Uylenburgh, a prominent art dealer.

♦ WINDMILLS
Wind power was used to pump water out of the areas enclosed by dikes.

♦ PROTECTING THE LAND
Amsterdam stands where the Ij and Amstel rivers flow together. In the early days of human settlement, a dam was built at this point. Later, the Dutch dug a dense network of canals to keep the sea from overrunning the land.

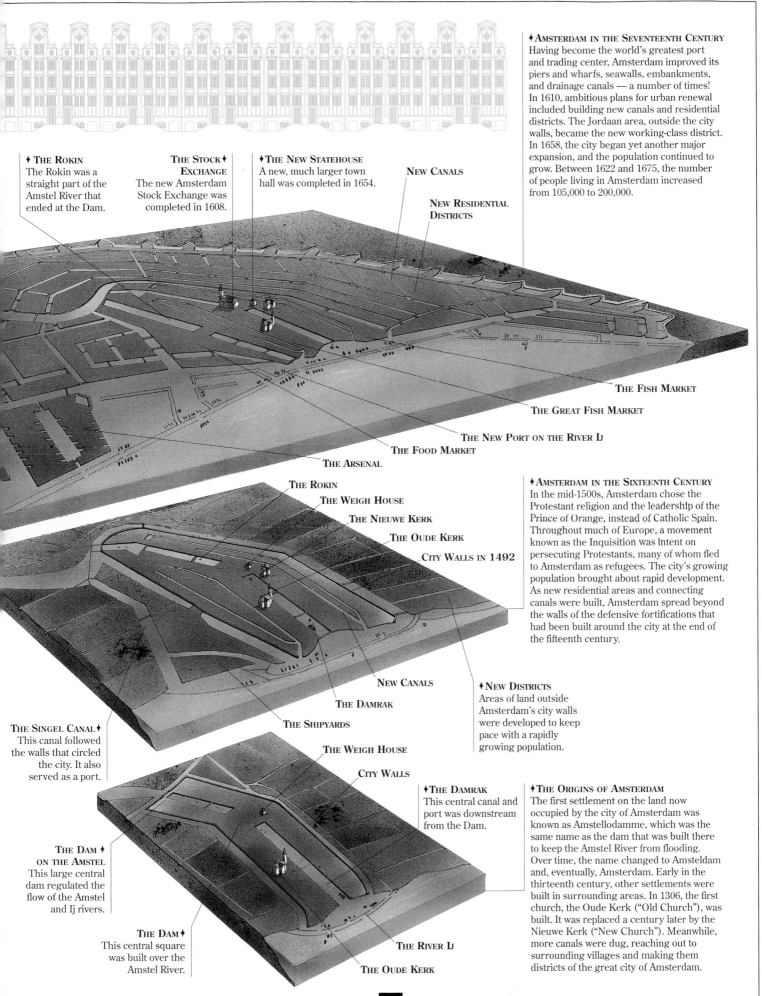

◆ **AMSTERDAM IN THE SEVENTEENTH CENTURY**
Having become the world's greatest port and trading center, Amsterdam improved its piers and wharfs, seawalls, embankments, and drainage canals — a number of times! In 1610, ambitious plans for urban renewal included building new canals and residential districts. The Jordaan area, outside the city walls, became the new working-class district. In 1658, the city began yet another major expansion, and the population continued to grow. Between 1622 and 1675, the number of people living in Amsterdam increased from 105,000 to 200,000.

◆ **THE ROKIN**
The Rokin was a straight part of the Amstel River that ended at the Dam.

THE STOCK ◆ EXCHANGE
The new Amsterdam Stock Exchange was completed in 1608.

◆ **THE NEW STATEHOUSE**
A new, much larger town hall was completed in 1654.

NEW CANALS

NEW RESIDENTIAL DISTRICTS

THE FISH MARKET

THE GREAT FISH MARKET

THE NEW PORT ON THE RIVER IJ

THE FOOD MARKET

THE ARSENAL

THE ROKIN

THE WEIGH HOUSE

THE NIEUWE KERK

THE OUDE KERK

CITY WALLS IN 1492

◆ **AMSTERDAM IN THE SIXTEENTH CENTURY**
In the mid-1500s, Amsterdam chose the Protestant religion and the leadership of the Prince of Orange, instead of Catholic Spain. Throughout much of Europe, a movement known as the Inquisition was intent on persecuting Protestants, many of whom fled to Amsterdam as refugees. The city's growing population brought about rapid development. As new residential areas and connecting canals were built, Amsterdam spread beyond the walls of the defensive fortifications that had been built around the city at the end of the fifteenth century.

NEW CANALS

THE DAMRAK

THE SHIPYARDS

◆ **NEW DISTRICTS**
Areas of land outside Amsterdam's city walls were developed to keep pace with a rapidly growing population.

THE SINGEL CANAL ◆
This canal followed the walls that circled the city. It also served as a port.

THE WEIGH HOUSE

CITY WALLS

◆ **THE DAMRAK**
This central canal and port was downstream from the Dam.

◆ **THE ORIGINS OF AMSTERDAM**
The first settlement on the land now occupied by the city of Amsterdam was known as Amstellodamme, which was the same name as the dam that was built there to keep the Amstel River from flooding. Over time, the name changed to Amsteldam and, eventually, Amsterdam. Early in the thirteenth century, other settlements were built in surrounding areas. In 1306, the first church, the Oude Kerk ("Old Church"), was built. It was replaced a century later by the Nieuwe Kerk ("New Church"). Meanwhile, more canals were dug, reaching out to surrounding villages and making them districts of the great city of Amsterdam.

THE DAM ◆ ON THE AMSTEL
This large central dam regulated the flow of the Amstel and Ij rivers.

THE DAM ◆
This central square was built over the Amstel River.

THE RIVER IJ

THE OUDE KERK

PORTRAIT PAINTING

Portraits became a distinct genre of painting in the fifteenth century. At the time, the Italian artists of the Renaissance tended to portray their subjects in an idealized way, while their Flemish contemporaries produced more realistic, down-to-earth portrayals. As portraits became fashionable in the royal courts of the sixteenth century, all the leading artists of the day began painting them. In the seventeenth century, the growth of wealthy middle classes, all seeking social advancement, significantly increased potential demand for portraits, and in Holland, a lively art market and the social climate of the young republic led to new developments in portrait painting. Already, in other parts of Europe, the desire to record a person's appearance for future generations was no longer limited to kings and queens or popes and other high-ranking clergy. By comparison, however, the call for portraits by the middle classes in Holland was strikingly greater than elsewhere. Another important aspect of Holland's portrait market was a change in attitude. In this independent, Calvinist country, individuals tended to be judged on merit and for the active roles they played in society, rather than on an assigned position, rank, or status. They wanted, therefore, to be portrayed as hard-working citizens or as members of established associations, social groups, or charitable organizations.

PORTRAITS OF
INDIVIDUALS
Artists from the city of Haarlem, known as the Haarlem school, were the first to excel in Dutch portrait painting. One of the greatest Haarlem artists was Frans Hals. In the mid-1600s, a more sophisticated form of portrait painting, as seen in the work of Anthony van Dyck, became fashionable in European courts.
1. Govaert Flinck (1615–1660), *Portrait of Rembrandt*, detail, c. 1636 (Rijksmuseum, Amsterdam)
2. Frans Hals, *Portrait of Nicolaes Hasselaer*, detail, c. 1635 (Rijksmuseum, Amsterdam)
3. Frans van Mieris (1635–1681), *Portrait of Woman with Parrot*, c. 1663 (National Gallery, London)
4. Attributed to Ferdinand Bol, *Portrait of Elisabeth Bas*, c. 1640 (Rijksmuseum, Amsterdam)
5. Gerard ter Borch (1617–1681), *Self-Portrait*, c. 1670 (Mauritshuis, The Hague)

1

2

GROUP PORTRAITS
1. Frans Hals, *Couple Out of Doors*, c. 1621 (Rijksmuseum, Amsterdam)
2. H. A. Pax, *The Princes of Orange in the Buitenhof at The Hague*, detail (Mauritshuis, The Hague)
3. Ferdinand Bol, *The Officers of the Wine Merchants Guild*, c. 1640 (Alte Pinakothek, Monaco)
4. Frans Hals, *Banquet of the Officers of the Militia Company of St. George*, 1616 (Frans Halsmuseum, Haarlem)
5. Jacob Lyon, *Captain Hoogkame's Company*, detail (Historisch Museum, Amsterdam)

1

2

5

5

♦ **FRANS HALS**
(c. 1580–1666)
Frans Hals joined
the Haarlem painters'
guild at the age of
twenty and soon
began specializing in
individual and group
portraits. His pictures
emphasized certain
facial features or a
few details of clothing,
while leaving the
setting vague and
undefined. Like his
younger colleague
Rembrandt, his style
contrasted with the
highly polished work
that was fashionable
elsewhere. In his
use of fresh, rapid
brushstrokes, Hals
was an innovator.

He also made an
important contribution
to group portraiture.
Instead of motionless,
posed compositions,
his group portrayals
give the impression
of movement in prog-
ress. The gestures of
his characters, how-
ever, are not always
coordinated as well as
those in Rembrandt's
group portraits.

♦ **THE DRINKER
AND THE FISHWIFE**
Two of Hals's most
famous images are
The Merry Drinker
(top), c. 1628
(Rijksmuseum,
Amsterdam) and
Hille Bobbe (above),
c. 1650 (Musée des
Beaux-Arts, Lille).

A PAIR OF PORTRAITS

With portraits in great demand, Rembrandt, although continuing his history painting, soon turned to portraiture. In portraying subjects, he was always careful to adapt the style of his work to the social role or position of the subject, such as clergyman, merchant, and so on. The portraits on these pages are painter Jacob de Gheyn III (1596–1641) and Secretary to the Dutch Council of State, Maurits Huygens (1595–1642).

SIGNS OF NOBILITY ✦
In contrast to the simplicity of Gheyn's and Huygens' portraits, this *Portrait of Maria Trip*, c. 1639 (Rijksmuseum, Amsterdam), contains many indications that the young woman portrayed came from a wealthy or noble family.

✦**REALISTIC FEATURES**
Rembrandt's skillful use of color produced lifelike facial features.

✦**DIGNIFIED SIMPLICITY**
While the subjects in the portraits appear refined, there is nothing fancy about their clothing, and the simple, neutral backgrounds give no suggestion of wealth or grandeur.

FREE AND NATURAL
Rembrandt used two main styles of painting in his portraiture. Increasingly, he preferred the use of free brushwork, producing a realistic effect by suggestion, in contrast to the more common style, which emphasized precision and a highly polished finish. The freer, more natural approach would become one of the identifying characteristics of Rembrandt's work.

✦ FREE BRUSHWORK
In Rembrandt's style of portrait painting, defining every outline and detail was not necessary to create the illusion of reality.

A POLISHED FINISH ✦
The style of portrait painting practiced throughout most of Europe in the 1600s relied on precision and polish, as in this detail from the Van Dyck portrait (far right).

✦ ANTHONY VAN DYCK
Portrait of a Man with His Son, 1628–1629 (Louvre, Paris), is a fine example of the polished style of Flemish painter Anthony van Dyck (1599–1641), who had once been a student of Peter Paul Rubens. Van Dyck's skill as a portrait artist was so highly regarded that his services were sought by courts in all parts of Europe.

✦ HANGING THE PORTRAITS
In Gheyn's portrait the light comes from the right, in Huygens', from the left. Rembrandt may have intended that the two portraits be hung on either side of a light source.

✦ PORTRAITS OF COUPLES
As the variety of Rembrandt's work increased, portraits of couples became a frequent theme. Usually, the subjects were married couples, as in these examples: *Portrait of Couple in an Interior* (top) 1633 (Isabella Stewart Gardner Museum, Boston), and *Portrait of a Seated Man* (bottom left), and *Portrait of a Seated Woman* (bottom right), both c. 1632 (Kunsthistorisches Museum, Vienna).

LAND OF FREEDOM

Seventeenth-century Holland was a land where people were relatively free to have different beliefs. Its atmosphere of tolerance was a big contributor to the nation's moral, intellectual, and economic development. Elsewhere in Europe, each state enforced its own brand of religion, and conflicting opinions were sometimes forcefully silenced. In contrast, Holland's republican form of government helped ensure personal freedom. Events in the year 1632 help show the difference between Holland and the rest of Europe. In that year, in France, heretics were burned at the stake. In Italy, the Inquisition forced Galileo to take back his support of the theory that the Sun is the center of the universe, which he had published in his *Dialogue Concerning the Two Chief World Systems*. Holland, in 1632, saw the births of artist Jan Vermeer; philosopher Baruch Spinoza, one of the greatest thinkers of his time; and scientist Antony van Leeuwenhoek, who invented the microscope.

✦ THE HOUSE OF ORANGE
Beginning in 1572 with William I, also known as "William the Silent," the leaders of the Dutch republic were members of the noble family of Orange. Today's Dutch monarchy still comes from a branch of the House of Orange. This engraving from 1672 (Historisch Museum, Rotterdam) features William III on horseback, surrounded by his predecessors (from left) William the Silent, Maurice, Frederick Henry, and William II.

✦ THE SYNOD OF DORDRECHT
In 1618 and 1619, the Dutch city of Dordrecht was the site of an important meeting that tried to settle differences of beliefs between two main groups of Calvinist Protestants, the conservative Gomarists and the liberal Arminians, who were hoping for tolerance. A scene of the meeting is represented in this engraving (Historisch Museum, Rotterdam).

REMBRANDT'S LIFE
While staying with Van Uylenburgh, Rembrandt met and fell in love with the art dealer's niece Saskia, who was the daughter of a wealthy judge in Friesland, one of Holland's northern provinces. Rembrandt married Saskia in July 1634. With his workshop and students already set up in the Van Uylenburgh household, the new couple stayed there, temporarily. Also in 1634, thanks to Constantijn Huygens, his friend and admirer in The Hague, Rembrandt received a major commission from Prince Frederick Henry to paint a series of pictures of Christ's passion.

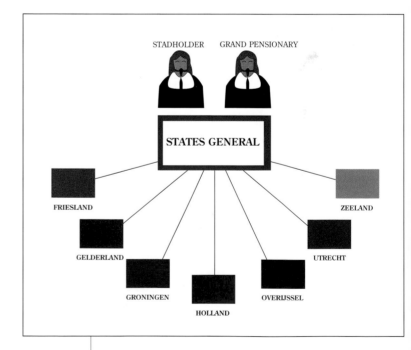

✦ THE DUTCH STATE
During the 1600s and 1700s, the United Provinces formed a complex republic made up of seven self-governing regions, of which Holland was the most important. The legislature, or body of lawmakers, called the States General, included representatives of both the middle classes and nobility. The two main leaders of the republic were the stadholder, or governor, who was also the head of the army, and the Grand Pensionary, a permanent, high-ranking official, who served as the chief minister of Holland.

✦ GALILEO
Italian astronomer and physicist Galileo Galilei (1564–1642) was famous for his experiments proving Copernicus's theory that Earth revolves around the Sun. In 1632, he published *Dialogue Concerning the Two Chief World Systems*, for which he was accused of heresy. As depicted by Joseph Nicolas Robert-Fleury (1797–1890) in *Galileo before the Inquisition, 1632*, 1847 (Louvre, Paris), Galileo was put on trial and was forced to deny his belief in the theory.

✦ BARUCH SPINOZA
Dutch philosopher Baruch Spinoza (1632–1677) was Jewish by birth, but his way of thinking offended both Jews and Christians, and he was forced to leave Amsterdam in 1656. In 1670, he published *Tractatus Theologico-Politicus*, which supported complete freedom of conscience, saying that no agency had the authority to interfere in matters of individual choice. Despite his great intellect, Spinoza chose to grind lenses for a living.

✦ WITCH HUNTS
In sixteenth- and seventeenth-century Europe, accusations of witchcraft were common, some made by people who were superstitious, others by the courts of the Inquisition in their eagerness to root out heresy. In Holland, the last witch was condemned in 1595. Elsewhere, witchcraft continued until the late 1700s. In 1632, in Loudun, France, Father Urbain Grandier, a Catholic priest, was accused of witchcraft by the nuns of a local convent and was burned at the stake.

✦ SOCIAL CONSCIENCE
The religious and moral values on which the Dutch republic was based made the work of establishing hospitals, orphanages, and institutions for the elderly matters of civic duty. These matters often found their way into works of art, such as *The Four Regents of the Leper Hospital* (left), 1649 (Historisch Museum, Amsterdam), by Ferdinand Bol, and *Distribution of Bread at the Almoezenierhuis* (right), 1627 (Historisch Museum, Amsterdam), by Werner van den Valckert (1585–1627).

SCIENCE AND PAINTING

In science and technology, as well as in the arts, Holland outpaced other European countries in the seventeenth century. At this time, great progress was being made in the field of optics, including improvements in manufacturing lenses and the development of the microscope. Holland became the main producer of lenses and was the birthplace of Antony van Leeuwenhoek, the inventor of the microscope. In some ways, art and science joined forces. The problem of visual perception, which was a concern of most artists, also interested many scientists. Art and science were also drawn together in the invention and use of the camera obscura. This instrument projected a real-world image onto a flat surface so the image could be traced. It eliminated an artist's need to use geometrical perspective to reproduce a scene. The realistic results achieved using a camera obscura can be seen in the paintings of Jan Vermeer.

♦ CANALETTO'S CAMERA OBSCURA
About a century after Vermeer, Venetian *vedutisti*, or "view painters," began using the camera obscura. *The Campo Santi Apostoli*, 1731–1735 (private collection, Milan), by Canaletto (1697–1768), is an example of a painting produced with the help of this device.

♦ CAMERA OBSCURA
The camera obscura was invented in the 1500s. Various kinds were made, but the most noteworthy were by Francesco Maurolico (1494–1575) in Italy and Johannes Kepler (1571–1630) in Germany. Dutch painters first used the device in the seventeenth century. In the eighteenth century, Venetian artists, such as Canaletto, used it to paint townscapes.

VERMEER'S ♦ CAMERA OBSCURA
For a television program, Philip Steadman, author of *Vermeer's Camera* (Oxford University Press, 2001), reconstructed the room in which Vermeer used a camera obscura.

A camera obscura, meaning "darkened chamber," consists of a dark room or box with a small hole cut into one wall. Light rays reflecting from a scene outside the wall travel through the hole, producing an upside-down image of the scene on the inside wall of the room or box, opposite the hole. Working in the dark, the camera operator would trace the shaky, indistinct image onto a sheet of paper. This principle was the basis for a number of ingenious models, both stationary and portable. In some models, the image was improved by the use of lenses and mirrors.

USING THE IMAGE ♦
The scenes for which Vermeer is believed to have used a camera obscura are all painted from the same viewpoint. The camera obscura would have been positioned at one end of a room. Vermeer would be inside it and would see, on its inside wall, an upside-down image of the scene at the opposite end of the room. He would trace the image as the basis, or outline, for his painting.

THE MAGIC BOX ✦
Rembrandt's student Samuel van Hoogstraten (1627–1678) became famous for his magic boxes, or "peep shows," such as this *View of the Interior of a Dutch House*, c. 1655–1660 (National Gallery, London). Cleverly assembled images and exaggerated perspective create the illusion of three-dimensional space.

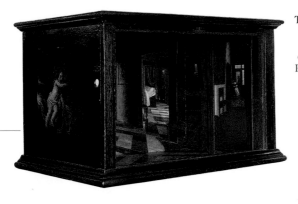

THE MUSIC LESSON ✦
Vermeer's painting *The Music Lesson*, c. 1664 (Buckingham Palace, London), was probably done in a room similar to the reconstructed room that appears below. Signs that a camera obscura was used include the almost photographic reflection of details in the foreground, the sparkling colors, and the realistic perspective.

LANDSCAPES

The large numbers of seventeenth-century Dutch landscape paintings found in art galleries, museums, and private collections today proves how popular this genre was in Holland at the time. Along with still lifes and everyday scenes, landscapes were valued possessions, hung in prominent places, to furnish the homes of middle-class Dutch families. Landscapes were also more affordable than other kinds of paintings. Dutch landscape artists did not use symbols with unclear meanings, trying to elevate their art. They simply produced natural and realistic pictures of the towns and countrysides in which they lived. These were the kinds of paintings the public preferred and purchased.

♦ A BIRD'S-EYE VIEW
View painting often came close to being cartography. *View of Amsterdam* (Historisch Museum, Amsterdam) is an extraordinarily skillful painting by Jan Christiaensz Micker (1660–1664), showing the city overshadowed by unseen clouds.

REMBRANDT'S LIFE
In 1635, Rembrandt and Saskia moved to another house. Rembrandt's business was growing, so he also had to look for a new workshop. He found an old warehouse he liked and transformed it to meet both his needs and the needs of his students, who had to live as well as work there. Rembrandt enjoyed a lavish lifestyle. The collections of paintings, engravings, and antiques he purchased led Saskia's family to accuse him of squandering his wife's wealth. Rembrandt saw these items as just part of his professional work.

CITY SCENES ♦ 1
"Lifelike" was the goal of any Dutch artist painting a city scene.

1. Jan van der Heyden (1637–1712), *View of the Town Hall*, 1668 (Louvre, Paris)
2. Jacob van Ruysdael (c. 1628–1682), *View of Haarlem*, c. 1670–1675 (Gemäldegalerie, Berlin)
3. Rembrandt, *View of Amsterdam*, 1640 (Rijksmuseum, Amsterdam)

WATER ♦ 1
Such a familiar element as water is rarely missing from a Dutch landscape.
1. Hendrick Cornelisz Vroom (c. 1563–1640), *The Port of Amsterdam*, detail, 1630 (Schlessheim Castle, Bavaria)
2. Salomon van Ruysdael (c. 1602–1670), *Landscape with River*, 1649 (Rijksmuseum, Amsterdam)
3. Willem van de Velde (1633–1707), *The Gouden Leeuw on the Ij at Amsterdam*, detail, 1686 (Historisch Museum, Amsterdam)

THE COUNTRYSIDE ♦ 1
Although the majority of Dutch citizens lived in cities or towns, they valued the land reclaimed from the sea and the marshes.
1. Herman van Swanevelt (c. 1600–1665), *Landscape with Figures*, detail, c. 1640 (Uffizi Gallery, Florence)
2. Paulus Potter, (1625–1654), *The Bull*, 1647 (Mauritshuis, The Hague)
3. Rembrandt, *Landscape with Bridge*, c. 1640 (Rijksmuseum, Amsterdam)

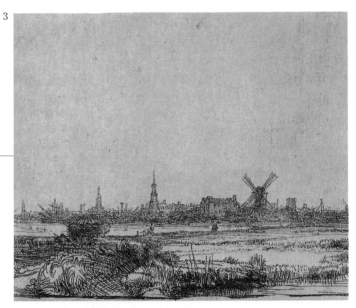

WINTER ✦
In *Winter Scene* (right), detail, c. 1608, (Rijksmuseum, Amsterdam), Hendrick Avercamp (1585–1684) depicts another common feature of Dutch landscape painting. Severe winters were typical of the Dutch climate, and many scenes of everyday life in winter show how the people of the Netherlands spent their time when normal work was at a standstill. A frozen canal, for example, prevented navigation and stopped trade.

THE ANATOMY LESSON

Sixteenth-century artists started the practice of setting a group portrait in an anatomy theater, which was a special room where students and other interested spectators could watch a corpse being dissected. The onlookers in Rembrandt's painting *The Anatomy Lesson of Dr. Nicolaes Tulp* are not medical men. They are local government officials who, as was customary in their day, are attending a lecture by a distinguished scientist, just as they might attend an important theater performance. The goal was to see and be seen.

DR. TULP ♦
Nicolaes Pietersz Tulp (1593–1657) was a lecturer in anatomy, appointed by the Amsterdam Guild of Surgeons in 1628. He also served two terms as burgomaster, or mayor, of the city.

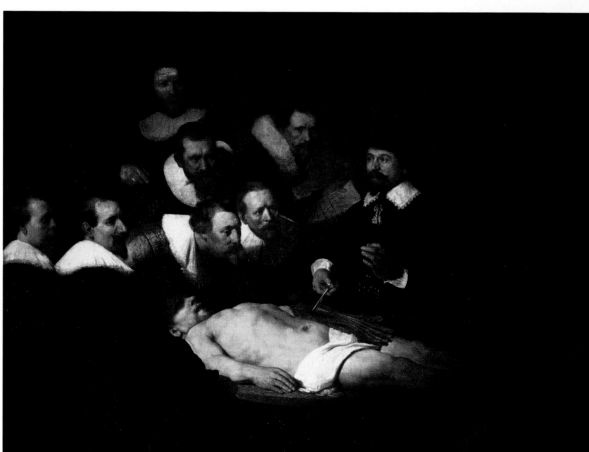

A FEELING OF UNITY

The Anatomy Lesson was Rembrandt's first test in the specific genre of group portrait painting, yet he was not afraid to deviate from traditional models. Instead of a stereotyped composition, with heads and bodies arranged on a single plane, he painted a lively, action-packed scene. With the noticeable interplay of glances and movements, he clearly tried to give the group a feeling of unity. This painting established Rembrandt's reputation and led him to quickly become one of Amsterdam's leading artists.

TULP'S GESTURE ♦
Rembrandt skillfully uses gesture to create a noticeable link between the surgeon and his audience. Dr. Tulp is using his left hand to demonstrate the action of the tendons in the fingers. At the same time, he uses the tweezers he is holding in his right hand to point to the tendons themselves.

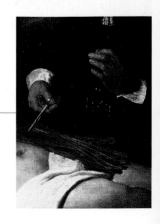

♦ FROM PAINTING TO THE MOVIES
Rembrandt was a master of atmosphere, and it seems that at least one film director has noticed. Compare the detail from the painting of Dr. Tulp's lecture (left) with a still shot from the 1943 film *Dies Irae* (right), made by German director Carl Theodor Dreyer. Rembrandt's influence could not be more obvious.

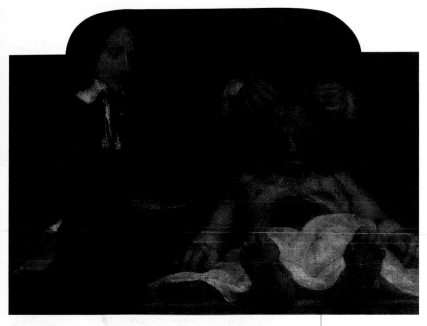

♦ MORE LESSONS
Pieter van Miereveld, *The Anatomy Lesson of Dr. Willem van der Meer* (above), 1617 (Gemeente Museum, Delft); Thomas de Keyser, *The Anatomy Lesson of Dr. Sebastiaen Egbertsz* (below), 1619 (Rijksmuseum, Amsterdam).

♦ ANOTHER LESSON
Rembrandt, *The Anatomy Lesson of Dr. Deyman*, 1656 (Historisch Museum, Amsterdam).

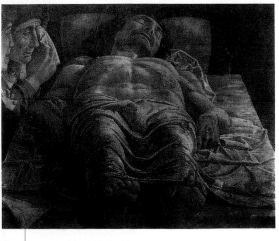

ANATOMY THEATER ♦
This engraving, 1644 (Bibliothèque Nationale, Paris), from Frederick Müller's *Atlas* shows the University of Leiden's famous anatomy theater, with a dissection in progress. In the mid-seventeenth century, lessons on anatomy were often open to the general public. In some cases, however, paying an entrance fee was required.

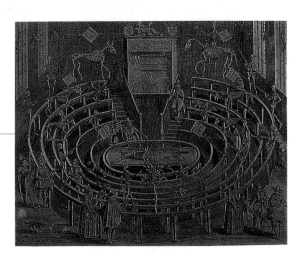

♦ AN ITALIAN MODEL
Much of Rembrandt's painting *The Anatomy Lesson of Dr. Deyman* was destroyed by fire in 1723. In a surviving fragment, however, the position of the corpse looks almost certainly modeled after the figure in *The Lamentation over the Dead Christ* (above), c. 1490 (Pinacoteca di Brera, Milan), by Andrea Mantegna (c. 1431–1506).

FOREIGN TRADE

From the sixteenth century's great voyages of discovery came widespread international trade. In the seventeenth century, European ships were traveling the world's oceans, far beyond the North, Baltic, and Mediterranean Seas. As workers from the southern provinces of the Netherlands came to Holland, Dutch shipping companies also began to travel the great ocean routes. From textiles and timber to herring, spices, and grains, the Dutch were involved in every kind of business, and their goods were in demand all over the world. Besides paying the laborers and sailors in Holland higher wages than anywhere else, the Dutch took full advantage of available capital and new, more efficient technology. With its growing import trade, cannon manufacturing, highly productive fishing industry, and other activities, Holland became the master of the seas. Two powerful businesses, the Dutch West India Company and the East India Company, were the agents of Dutch sea power.

✦ HEAVY ARTILLERY

Due to the ongoing conflict between Spain and the Netherlands, the Dutch needed to arm their ships with heavy weapons, which encouraged them to become involved in cannon manufacturing. Sixteenth-century cannons needed to be improved. In the 1500s, one-piece barrels were still unknown, so manufacturers made cannon barrels in two pieces that had to be clamped together, and they were uncertain about the best metal to use. Brass was a high-quality metal but very expensive. Iron cost less but was considered inferior. Because Dutch cannons were actually made in Sweden, Dutch businessmen shrewdly profited from that country's iron ore and timber resources.

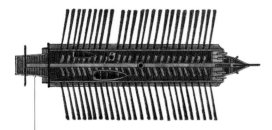

✦ THE GALLEY

In the sixteenth century, a great deal of merchandise was still carried on the Mediterranean in galleys, which were ships with banks of oars, typically rowed by prisoners. Galleys were also used in battle, but they became outdated as ocean-going galleons took to the sea.

✦ THE GALLEON

For all of the sixteenth century and part of the seventeenth, the most important sailing ship was the galleon. Besides having two decks and three masts, a galleon was usually outfitted for war and carried powerful cannons. In 1588, English galleons easily defeated the ships of the Spanish Armada.

THE DUTCH FLUYT ✦

In 1595, a new type of ship appeared in Dutch ports. The three-masted ship was called a "fluyt," and it was fast. It could also navigate in shallow water and could be handled by a small crew. Its rounded shape, bulging sides, and unusually small deck gave the fluyt two big advantages. It could carry a lot of cargo, and it also limited the amount of tax that had to be paid for using the Sund, which was a narrow strait between Denmark and Scandinavia. Every ship had to pay a tax to pass through the Sund. The amount of the tax was based on the size of the ship's deck.

♦ OCEAN TRADE
Dutch ships began
traveling ocean
trade routes in
the late sixteenth
century. The earliest
voyages were in the
Baltic, North, and
Mediterranean Seas.
Later, they included
the whole world,
from South America
to India to Japan.

♦ THE EAST INDIA COMPANY
The Dutch East India Company was
founded in 1602, when the conflict
between Spain and the United Provinces
was at its height. To defend their ships
and their businesses, shipping companies
and merchants formed an alliance, to
which the Dutch government gave
powers to negotiate, trade, arm soldiers,
and establish military posts in lands east
of the Cape of Good Hope, which is the
southernmost tip of Africa. During the
seventeenth century, the East India
Company became the world's most powerful commercial organization.
In Europe, its headquarters were in
Amsterdam (above). In the east, its
center of operations was Batavia, now
called Jakarta, which is the capital and
largest city of Indonesia and is at the
heart of the Dutch East Indies. Sailing in
large groups, or convoys, the East India
Company's ships carried spices, cotton
fabrics, porcelain, tea, gold, and diamonds.
Voyages lasted months, even years,
and many of those who set sail died on
the voyage or chose not to return home.
Toward the end of the century, the
East India Company suffered financial dif-
ficulties, and in 1799, it was dissolved.

THE COUNSELLOR ♦
In 1631, Philips
Lucasz was appointed
Counsellor General,
or main lawyer,
for the East India
Company. Rembrandt
painted Lucasz's
portrait (right)
in 1635.

CARTOGRAPHY

To seventeenth-century Europeans, the shapes of countries and of the world were very similar to the way we see them today. Even four centuries ago, relatively accurate maps were already widely available. Those maps, however, were more correct in representing better-known areas, such as big cities and coastlines near major ports, than they were in showing the features of distant and unexplored territories.

As navigation developed, so did the need for more precision in planning voyages. With advancements in drawing and measurement techniques came constant improvements in the quality of maps. In the seventeenth century, cartography, or mapmaking, developed hand in hand with book publishing, and Holland was the leading producer of maps and nautical charts.

♦ MAPS AS DECORATION
In Dutch homes of the 1600s, maps were often part of the furnishings. They can be seen displayed as wall decorations in many paintings of interior scenes, including *The Artist's Studio*, c. 1665 (Kunsthistorisches Museum, Vienna), by Jan Vermeer. A detail of this painting is shown above.

♦ MAPS OF THE HEAVENS
Along with land maps and globes, Dutch mapmakers also produced planispheres and maps of the night sky. An image of a celestial globe, a globe that charted the heavens, appears in Vermeer's *The Astronomer*, 1668 (Louvre, Paris). Jocodus Hondius built a globe of this kind (left), 1600 (Nederlands Historisch Scheepvaartsmuseum, Amsterdam).

♦ A MAJOR ACHIEVEMENT IN CARTOGRAPHY
In the forty-five-year period from 1572 to 1617, Georg Braun (1541–1622), a German clergyman, and a cartographer named Frans Hogenberg (c. 1536–1590) completed a huge mapmaking project. Called *Civitates Orbis Terrarum*, which means "Cities of the Earth," it was the first organized attempt to represent as maps the major cities of Europe, the African coast, and the Near East. To make the 531 plates in this work, Braun and Hogenberg joined forces with hundreds of cartographers, draftsmen, engravers, public officials, and individual citizens, who supplied both plans for and information about their native cities. The work was an outstanding success. For the first time, navigators, merchants, and ordinary travelers had a reference guide that showed the main buildings, access routes, gates, and fortifications of each city. Information about the customs and dress of the inhabitants of each city was also included in the work. The image above is the plate of Amsterdam in 1572, which appeared in Volume I.

♦ RYTHER'S THEODOLITE
Manufactured in 1590 by Augustine Ryther (c. 1550–1593) of London, this theodolite (Museo di Storia della Scienza, Florence) is the oldest example of its kind.

THE SIGHTS ♦
The theodolite's original gun-type sights were replaced by a telescope in the eighteenth century.

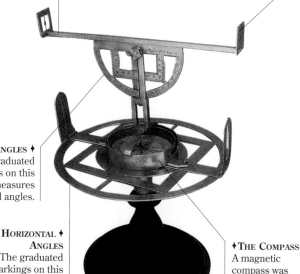

VERTICAL ANGLES ♦
The graduated markings on this semicircle measures vertical angles.

HORIZONTAL ♦ ANGLES
The graduated markings on this flat circle measures horizontal angles.

♦ THE COMPASS
A magnetic compass was incorporated into the theodolite.

♦ MEASURING INSTRUMENTS
The development of cartography in the 1600s would not have been possible if progress had not also been made in the development of instruments for measuring. A device called a theodolite was, undoubtedly, the most imprtant new invention. It enabled a user to measure the angles between three different points on the ground. When the length of one side of the triangle formed by the points was known, the user could calculate the lengths of the other two sides.

♦ TOPOGRAPHY INSTRUMENTS
To accurately draw the features of a place or
an area on a map, a topographer would have
used the kinds of instruments contained in
this leather case dating from the middle of
the seventeenth century (Museo di Storia
della Scienza, Florence). They include
pencils, rulers, and pairs of compasses, for
measuring distances and drawing circles.

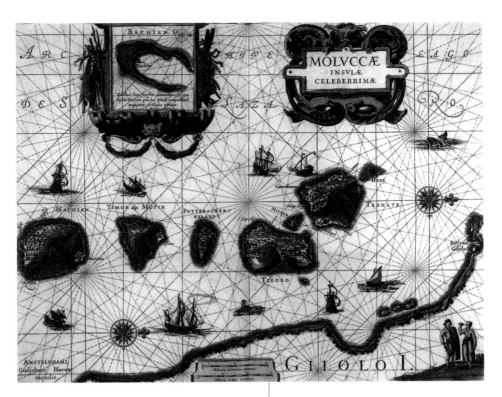

♦ THE MOLUCCAS
Reliable new maps were essential for shipping
companies, and the East India Company was
one of a Dutch mapmaker's main customers.
In 1607, the Dutch took possession of the
Moluccas, a group of islands in the Pacific
Ocean that became very important to spice
traders. Dutch mapmaker Jan Jansson (1588–
1664) made this very decorative map of the
Moluccas in 1647.

♦ VERMEER'S GEOGRAPHER
Jan Vermeer's famous painting *The Geographer*, 1669
(Städelsches Kunstinstitut, Frankfurt), shows a man using
a pair of compasses to measure distances on a map. The
picture also includes other cartographic items, including a
globe on top of the cupboard and a framed map hanging on
the wall. Art scholars have noticed that the same features of
this man's face appear in other paintings by Vermeer. Some
scholars think they are the features of the artist himself.

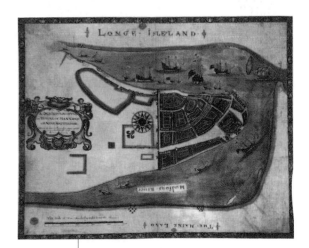

♦ MANHATTAN
In the sixteenth century, Italian explorer
Giovanni da Verrazano (1485–1528) came upon
a peninsula in North America that was called
"Mannahatta" by the Algonquin Indians who
lived there. The Dutch purchased the land in
1626 and established a colony called Nieuw
("New") Amsterdam. Pieter ("Peter") Stuyvesant
(c. 1602–1672) was the Dutch Director-General,
or governor, of New Amsterdam from 1647
to 1664, when the town fell into British hands
and was renamed New York. This map of the
area from 1664 (British Library, London) was
presented to the Duke of York. The creator of
the map is unknown.

VERMEER

Jan Vermeer was not well-known in his lifetime. In fact, his scenes remained unnoticed by art scholars until the beginning of the twentieth century. Along with Rembrandt, Vermeer is now seen as the other outstanding Dutch painter of the 1600s. While Rembrandt, however, was a very productive painter, no more than thirty-five authenticated works by Vermeer are known today.

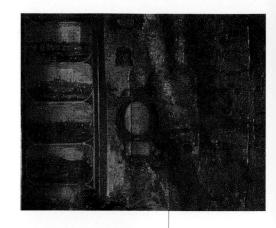

♦ VERMEER'S LIFE
Not much is known about Vermeer's career or personality, but a great deal is known about his parents and his family's financial affairs. Their story includes the difficult circumstances, broken promises, unpaid debts, creditors, court cases, and failed business ventures that are all too familiar in the lives of Dutch artists.

Jan Vermeer was born in Delft in 1632. His father was a textile worker, an innkeeper, and, on occasion, an art dealer. Vermeer continued to run his father's inn and deal in art but was not very successful. Nothing is known about how he learned to paint, except that he was already enrolled in the artists' guild at the age of twenty-one. In 1653, he married Catharina Bolnes, who was from a Catholic family and was socially superior to Vermeer.

♦ VERMEER'S ART
A detail of the woman's face from *The Artist's Studio* appears at the top of this column. The thumbnail above is *The Geographer*, 1669 (Städelsches Kunstinstitut, Frankfurt).

♦ THE MAP
Maps hung like paintings in Dutch houses of the 1600s. The maps seen in many of Vermeer's works have been interpreted as his way of pointing out that both painters and cartographers are descriptive artists.

♦ THE CURTAIN
In Vermeer's scene, the curtain, much like a theater curtain, separates spectators from role players.

♦ EVERYDAY OBJECTS
Careful examination of Vermeer's works reveals everyday objects that, put together, would recontruct the furnishings and decor of his house.

VERMEER'S PRIVATE WORLD
Jan Vermeer painted interiors or, perhaps, only one interior. Most of his paintings appear to be set in a single room, probably in his own house. His scenes portray an atmosphere of silence and suspense. The setting in *The Artist's Studio*, c. 1665, is typical of his private world, which seems haunted by mysterious figures and reappearing objects.

♦ WOMAN WITH A PEARL NECKLACE
c. 1662–1665
(Gemäldegalerie, Berlin). Vermeer's paintings reveal even the contents of the family wardrobe. In this painting, the yellow silk jacket edged with ermine is precisely described in the inventory of belongings that was drawn up after Vermeer died.

WOMAN READING ♦ A LETTER
c. 1662–1663
(Rijksmuseum, Amsterdam). Reading and writing are activities that appear frequently in Vermeer's paintings, magnifying the mysterious silence that seems to surround many of his subjects. Also seen again in this painting is the familiar map.

♦ FAMILY MATTERS
In marrying a Catholic woman, Vermeer apparently had no guilt about abandoning his Calvinist beliefs. He married Catharina only two weeks after their engagement. During his marriage, Vermeer fathered fifteen children, although four of them died as infants. Taking care of a large family was not easy.

♦ A LADY STANDING AT A VIRGINAL
1670 (National Gallery, London). An elegantly dressed lady stands before a virginal, a small musical instrument similar to the harpsichord.

DELFT ♦
Although most of Vermeer's paintings are interior scenes, *View of Delft*, c. 1660–1661 (Mauritshuis, The Hague), is one of art's most impressive cityscapes.

♦ THE GLASS OF WINE
c. 1658–1661
(Gemäldegalerie, Berlin). In this picture, as in other interior scenes by Vermeer, the perspective effects seem to indicate that the artist typically used a fixed camera obscura when painting interiors. A detail from *The Glass of Wine* is shown below.

♦ VERMEER'S DEATH
Catharina's mother did all she could to help her daughter and son-in-law. In 1675, however, when he was only forty-three years old, Vermeer died. Two years later, Catharina wrote these words about her husband's death: "Because the children were a great burden, and because we lacked financial means, he fell into such a depression and lethargy that he lost his health in the space of a day and a half, and died." After Vermeer's death, most of his paintings were sold to pay off his debts.

HOMES AND HOUSES

Simplicity and good taste best describe the household furnishings in Calvinist Holland. Seventeenth-century Dutch paintings provide a clear idea of how Dutch homes looked inside. Bedrooms contained large wardrobes made of solid wood; kitchen tables were always close to a window, the main source of light; floors were paved with large glazed or terra-cotta tiles; and pictures decorated plain walls. Outside, houses were often crowned with stair-step style gables. There were, of course, considerable differences between the houses of the rich and the poor. Not everyone, in fact, had a house. Amsterdam attracted many unemployed foreigners who lived without roofs over their heads. The fortunate ones might live in a basement or a wooden shed. Going up the social scale, some people lived in modest houses built on narrow plots of ground, others in comfortable "double dwellings" or, possibly, aristocratic town houses.

✦ REMBRANDT'S HOUSE
The house Rembrandt lived in from 1639 to 1658 still stands on the part of St. Anthoniesbreestraat known as Jodenbreestraat. The house became a museum in 1911.

ROPES AND ✦ PULLEYS
Most Dutch town houses had a rope and pulley attached to the front of the gable for lifting furniture and other heavy loads to the upper levels.

NEW GABLES ✦
Bell-shaped gables became fashionable in about 1660.

FACADES ✦
The narrow facades, or faces, of medieval buildings had simple, triangular gables. Stair-step style gables did not appear until the sixteenth century.

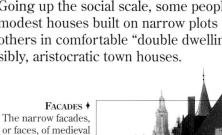

REMBRANDT'S LIFE

On May 1, 1639, Rembrandt and Saskia moved into a large house on St. Anthoniesbreestraat ("St. Anthony's Broad Street") in the center of Amsterdam. In 1641, Saskia gave birth to a son, Titus. Saskia died the following year, and a widow named Geertje Dircx came to live in the house as Titus's nurse. Although Rembrandt developed a relationship with Geertje, he never married her, and by 1649, the relationship had fallen apart. Geertje sued Rembrandt for breaking his promise of marriage, and Rembrandt was ordered to pay her an annual allowance. Meanwhile, Rembrandt formed a relationship with Hendrickje Stoffels, a young girl who also worked for him. He couldn't marry her without losing the benefits of Saskia's will, but they indulged their extravagant tastes together, piling one debt on top of another.

✦ CANAL ACCESS
Almost every house in Amsterdam and other large cities opened onto one of the main waterways. Most families kept a boat anchored near their home.

♦ WINDOWS
The front of the house had large windows. On the middle stories, the top panes of the windows were often fixed in place and could not be opened.

♦ HOIST
In addition to the rope and pulley on the front of the gable, many houses had a hoist in the attic for lifting heavy loads.

THE ROOF ♦
A steeply pitched roof was hidden behind the gable of the house. The roof was made of wooden timbers that were covered with wavy-edged, interlocking tiles (far right).

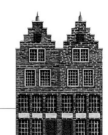

♦ THE ATTIC
Most stored goods were kept in the attic of a Dutch home. The attic was usually dry and was less accessible to rats and mice than the cellar.

♦ BEDROOMS
The bedrooms were located on the upper floors. Most were furnished with large, four-poster beds.

♦ THE LIVING ROOM
The main entrance and reception room were on the ground floor, which was slightly above street level.

♦ THE STAIRCASE
A wooden staircase connected the floors of the house, from the ground level to the attic, rising in a spiral through the center of the house.

♦ THE KITCHEN
The kitchen was at the back of the house, at approximately ground level.

♦ THE PANTRY
Some houses had a storage pantry either next to or beneath the kitchen.

♦ THE CELLAR
The area below street level was used for storing goods that did not need a dry environment.

♦ FOUNDATIONS
When brick started to replace wood as a building material, new buildings were heavier than in the past, and stronger foundations were needed to support them. Hundreds of tall, thick wooden poles, called piles, were driven as deep as 36 feet (11 meters) into the ground.

♦ CHANGING STYLES
In the Middle Ages, houses had simple, triangular gables, but, as time went by, more elaborate styles became fashionable. Some typical styles of the seventeenth century were bell-shaped gables and gables with a central rectangle that was narrower then the building's facade.

♦ CHANGING MATERIALS
Most Dutch houses in the Middle Ages were made of wood. After a series of disastrous fires in the 1400s, however, city officials were convinced that wood should be banned as a building material, and brick should be used instead. From 1452, the side walls of houses had to be brick. Wood was still permitted for facades until 1669, after which its use was forbidden by law, but by that time, wood was generally being used only for roof timbers. When Amsterdam's old Town Hall burned down in 1652, Rembrandt was fascinated by the ruins and made a drawing of them.

Genre Paintings

Some art historians call paintings of scenes from daily life "genre paintings." For the people of seventeenth-century Holland, who all seemed to like paintings of interiors, genre paintings were particular favorites. What was it about interior paintings that the Dutch found so appealing? They saw themselves in these pictures, as well as their houses, possessions, and activities. The people in the paintings were unknown, so anyone could identify with them. Calvinism considered thrift and hard work religious virtues, and, to the Dutch, these paintings seemed to reflect prosperity gained by obedience to the teachings of the Bible. Max Friedländer, a German art historian, wrote, "Genre was particularly popular in the north, where the republican Dutch, within their narrow, victoriously defended borders, viewed their secure existence with a sense of satisfaction." The academic artists and art connoisseurs of Europe felt that paintings worthy of the name "genre" should feature heroes, saints, or gods. In their view, a scene of daily life reflected the tastes of an uncultured middle class. Nevertheless, a considerable number of great artists devoted themselves to genre painting. Today, these paintings are seen as works of beauty and valuable sources of information about the social life of the past.

♦ Firefighters at Work
This engraving by Jan van der Heyden shows firefighters at work on a blazing house. The engraving comes from Van der Heyden's book *Brandspitenboeck*, or "Fire Engine Book," 1690 (Historisch Museum, Amsterdam). The artist was both a genre painter and a fire chief.

Tavern Interiors ♦
Fierce competition, along with the low prices placed on genre paintings, gradually led artists to specialize in and become known for certain subjects. The interior tavern scenes of Jan Steen (1626–1679) (right) show the almost chaotic liveliness that characterized Steen's works.

1. *The Cabaret*, c. 1660–1670 (Mauritshuis, The Hague)
2. *The Prince's Birthday*, 1660 (Rijksmuseum, Amsterdam)

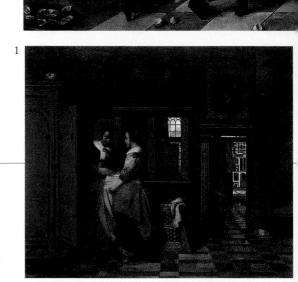

Daily Life ♦
1. Pieter de Hooch (1629–1684), *The Linen Cupboard*, 1663 (Rijksmuseum, Amsterdam)
2. Adriaen van Ostade (1610–1685), *Country Party*, 1661 (Rijksmuseum, Amsterdam)
3. Pieter de Hooch, *Drinkers in the Bower*, 1658 (National Gallery of Scotland, Edinburgh)
4. Frans van Mieris, *Two Old People at Table*, c. 1655–1660 (Uffizi, Florence)

Church Interiors ♦
Some genre painters were inspired by the solemn architecture of Dutch Protestant churches, others by Catholic churches or Jewish synagogues. Pieter Saenredam (1597–1665) and Emanuel de Witte (c. 1617–1692) were two such artists.

1. Pieter Saenredam, *Interior of St. Lawrence Church at Alkmaar*, 1661 (Boymans, Rotterdam)
2. Emanuel de Witte, *Church Interior*, 1617–1622 (Musée Jeanne d'Aboville, La Fere)
3. Pieter Saenredam, *Interior of the Church of St. Bavo at Haarlem*, 1636 (Rijksmuseum, Amsterdam)

2

3

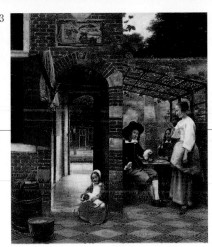

4

3

THE REMBRANDT FAMILY

Rembrandt had at least two lengthy relationships with women he never married. He also fathered a child outside of marriage. His nonconformist attitude toward marriage gives us some idea of what he thought of himself and his relationship with society. It seems clear that Rembrandt could not stand rules and regulations. He may have had the view that his status as an artist excused him from the same standards of behavior as ordinary citizens. In general, Rembrandt earned the moral disapproval of society. He was also criticized for his casual attitude toward money and his failure to settle his debts. His extravagance in buying all kinds of paintings, furniture, and collectors' items was the direct opposite of thrift, a virtue of great importance to Calvinists.

✦ REMBRANDT'S MOTHER
Cornelia Willemsdr van Zuytbroeck was probably the model for the elderly women in her son's early works. *Rembrandt's Mother as the Prophetess Anna*, 1631 (Rijksmuseum, Amsterdam).

✦ REMBRANDT'S FATHER
This portrait of Harmen Gerritsz van Rijn seems to reflect his status as a successful and fairly wealthy man. Rembrandt was the eighth of his nine children. *Rembrandt's Father*, c. 1630–1631 (Mauritshuis, The Hague).

SASKIA ✦
Rembrandt married Saskia in 1634. They had one son, Titus, born in 1641. Saskia died in 1642. *Saskia van Uylenburgh in Arcadian Costume*, 1635 (National Gallery, London).

HENDRICKJE ✦
Rembrandt lived with Hendrickje Stoffels from about 1648 until her death in 1663. *Portrait of Hendrickje Stoffels*, c. 1650–1654 (Louvre, Paris).

REMBRANDT'S LIFE

In 1654, the church charged Rembrandt and Hendrickje of living together without being married, but the couple did not appear before the courts. Later, Hendrickje appeared alone and was ordered to repent. That same year, she gave birth to a daughter, Cornelia. Rembrandt's debts continued to grow, and he sold very few paintings. By 1656, he was bankrupt. Titus, who was the beneficiary of his mother's estate, made a will, leaving his property to Hendrickje and Cornelia, but the will also allowed Rembrandt to enjoy the property during his lifetime. Nothing, however, could save Rembrandt's collections of art, furniture, books, and theatrical costumes from being auctioned in 1657 and 1658.

✦ DRAWING OF SASKIA
Rembrandt's wife was the subject of both drawings and paintings. This drawing was probably done only a year or two before Saskia died.

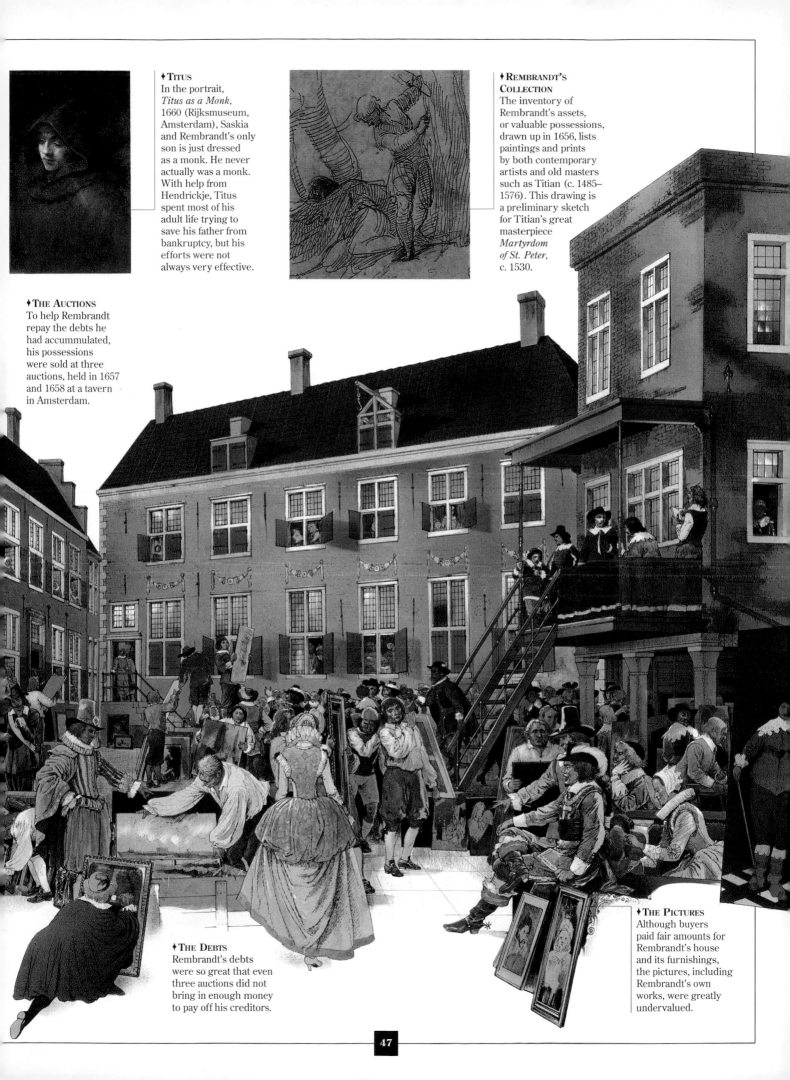

✦**TITUS**
In the portrait, *Titus as a Monk*, 1660 (Rijksmuseum, Amsterdam), Saskia and Rembrandt's only son is just dressed as a monk. He never actually was a monk. With help from Hendrickje, Titus spent most of his adult life trying to save his father from bankruptcy, but his efforts were not always very effective.

✦**REMBRANDT'S COLLECTION**
The inventory of Rembrandt's assets, or valuable possessions, drawn up in 1656, lists paintings and prints by both contemporary artists and old masters such as Titian (c. 1485–1576). This drawing is a preliminary sketch for Titian's great masterpiece *Martyrdom of St. Peter*, c. 1530.

✦**THE AUCTIONS**
To help Rembrandt repay the debts he had accummulated, his possessions were sold at three auctions, held in 1657 and 1658 at a tavern in Amsterdam.

✦**THE DEBTS**
Rembrandt's debts were so great that even three auctions did not bring in enough money to pay off his creditors.

✦**THE PICTURES**
Although buyers paid fair amounts for Rembrandt's house and its furnishings, the pictures, including Rembrandt's own works, were greatly undervalued.

THE WORKSHOP

Like the workshops of other Dutch artists of the period, Rembrandt's workshop served as a school as well as a production studio. His students came to him at about the age of fifteen, many of them from other towns and cities. They lived, worked, studied, and slept in the workshop. Contracts that have survived the years show that Rembrandt charged the parents or guardians of his students high fees for their training and room and board. The workshop was essentially a business. Paintings produced by the students later in their training were sold by the master, who would often sign his own name to them. And the master's word was law. He dictated the subject matter, styles, and prices of his students' works.

♦THE PAINTER'S
STUDIO
Rembrandt did
this engraving
(Louvre, Paris)
in about 1648.

LIGHTING ♦
Large windows
were essential in an
artist's workshop,
which needed plenty
of natural light.

ATMOSPHERE ♦
In the studio, the
master and his
students usually
worked together on
the same subject.
Many of their
sketches and
drawings provided
information about
the atmosphere of
the workshop.

REMBRANDT'S LIFE

In 1660, with his talent being recognized by painters and poets alike, Rembrandt signed a contract with Titus and Hendrickje, giving them, and only them, the right to sell any works he had produced until seven years after his death. In exchange, they guaranteed Rembrandt free room and board. Although the family had to leave the large house and workshop in the center of the city for a smaller dwelling in the working-class district, the agreement still had many advantages. For some time, Titus and Hendrickje had been running their own art business. The agreement put them first in line among Rembrandt's creditors and the first, over any others, to be able to make a claim. For his part, Rembrandt could continue painting in peace.

♦ DRAPERY
An artist's workshop always had a variety of fabrics that could be hung or draped over a frame or a dummy for the students to copy.

♦ MODELS
Using real people as models, even nude models, was just part of the normal practice of drawing from life. Usually the models were people from the city's lower classes, but friends and relatives, and even the students themselves, would sometimes stand in.

SCREENS ♦
Folding screens were set up in the workshop to give students, and even the master, more isolated work areas for studies that required a lot of concentration.

♦ STUDY MATERIALS
Rembrandt's obsession with costumes and collectibles might explain some of the materials in his workshop, such as statues, armor, and unusual headgear.

♦ PAINTS
Rembrandt prepared his paints with great care. He often used expensive new pigments, which had to be crushed or ground into powder before mixing them with water or oil to make paints.

♦ THE WORK
The Night Watch,
1642, oil on canvas,
143 x 172 inches
(363 x 437 cm),
(Rijksmuseum,
Amsterdam). Known
also as *The Company
of Frans Banning
Cocq and Willem van
Ruytenburch*, this
group portrait may
be Rembrandt's most
famous painting.

THE NIGHT WATCH

The names of eighteen people in this group portrait are known. They include musketeers of the Amsterdam Civic Guard with their captain, Frans Banning Cocq. The painting also includes a number of unknown bystanders along with the eighteen known subjects.

♦ THE CAPTAIN
Frans Banning Cocq (1605–1655) was a son-in-law of the mayor of Amsterdam. He was a wealthy and ambitious man who knew the value of his military rank. Amsterdam's citizen militias played a key role in the war against Spain.

It was commissioned in 1638, when a number of artists, including Rembrandt, were asked to paint group portraits of Amsterdam's militia companies for the visit of French queen Marie de Médicis.

DAY BECOMES NIGHT

Instead of showing his subjects standing in a row or around a table, Rembrandt used lighting, color, and depth to create a lively, natural-looking scene. He painted the scene as taking place in daylight, but in the 1700s, the painting came to be called *The Night Watch*, and the name stuck.

♦ A FACE IN THE CROWD
At the back of the crowd, the partially hidden face, peering over the shoulder of the man holding the flag, might possibly represent the artist himself.

✦ THE MUSKET

As a characteristic weapon of a militia, the musket is a prominent feature in *The Night Watch*. A soldier on the left is loading his musket; a soldier behind the captain appears to be firing his; and another soldier, to the right, is blowing into the chamber of his gun after firing it.

✦ USE OF COLOR

Rembrandt's use of color produces some extraordinary effects of light and shade. The placement of light and dark colors and the subtle variations of tone create a rich, dense atmosphere. Also impressive is the skillful perspective Rembrandt uses to make the lance look as if it is projecting outward.

✦ A WORK BEYOND COMPARE

Even after the size of the painting had been cut down (see text lower right), the picture still included twenty-eight men, three children, and a dog. The names of the known characters appear in the background, on a large shield above the corner of the archway, which was added after Rembrandt's death. These individuals had all made a contribution to the fee Rembrandt was paid for the painting. The subjects closer to the front paid more. The portrait was almost instantly famous. Samuel van Hoogstraten, who was a student of Rembrandt's, wrote: "This work will outshine all its rivals. It is conceived with such painterly insight, so full of dramatic movement and so powerfully executed, that similar paintings seem like playing cards by comparison."

✦ DAYLIGHT SCENE

Rembrandt's group portrait of Captain Frans Banning Cocq and the Civic Guard was intended to hang in the Amsterdam headquarters of the musketeers. It was removed from that location, however, in 1715, and was trimmed down so it would fit in a smaller room at the Amsterdam town hall. The watercolor above (from a book by Jacob Cats, which is kept with other seventeenth- and eighteenth-century copies in the Rijksmuseum in Amsterdam) shows what Rembrandt's original painting looked like. It also confirms that *The Night Watch* was originally set in daylight. Dirt and grime settling into the painting's canvas, and, possibly, the role of the Civic Guard changing to a nighttime security patrol, may have created the impression that the painting was a night scene, leading to the widespread use of its more familiar, but inappropriate, title.

ETCHING

Making multiple copies of a single picture lowers both the cost of production and the purchase price. The business-minded artists of seventeenth-century Holland were well aware of this fact. They became experts in the technique of etching, which enabled them to make large numbers of prints from one original painting. The prints could then be widely distributed, publicizing the artist's work. Because prints were fairly inexpensive, they found their way into almost every Dutch home and became the preferred medium for subjects with popular appeal, such as calendars, caricatures, and stories. Producing prints quickly led to putting pictures in periodicals, the forerunners of modern newspapers.

♦ A WOODCUT
First practiced in Europe in the 1300s, a woodcut is the oldest technique for reproducing an image as a print. The artist cut into a block of soft wood, leaving the image in relief, or raised above the surface of the wood. The image was then inked and printed onto paper.

♦ AN ENGRAVING
Reproductions, or prints, known as engravings first appeared in the late 1400s. Instead of a relief cut on a block of wood, an image was "scratched" onto a metal plate. It could be line-engraved, either by cutting the metal surface with a sharp, pointed blade or by drawing with a steel needle. The image could also be etched into the plate using acid. The process of etching plates to produce engravings is described on these pages.

♦ WOODCUT ARTIST
The *Portrait of Willibald Pirkheimer*, 1524 (above), is a woodcut by German artist Albrecht Dürer (1471–1528). After learning the basics of engraving from his father, who was a goldsmith, Dürer became highly skilled at woodcuts and line engravings.

4. BLACKENING ♦
The surface of the plate that will have the drawing on it is held over a flame until smoke from the flame colors the entire surface an intense black.

1. THE PLATE ♦
The thin metal plate used to make an engraving is usually copper. It is only .04 to .08 inches (1 or 2 millimeters) thick and has a mirror-smooth surface.

2. PREPARING ♦ THE PLATE
The plates edges are filed smooth, so they do not cut the paper during printing, and its surface is cleaned with a chalk solution.

5. DRAWING THE IMAGE ♦
A steel needle is used to draw the image on the plate. The artist can draw directly on the blackened wax surface, but the more common method is to trace over a drawing already done on paper. In either case, the steel needle delicately cuts into the wax, exposing the metal beneath it.

♦ 3. WAXING
A brush is used to spread a thin layer of liquid wax onto each side of the plate.

6. ACID ETCHING ♦
The plate is immersed in an acid solution that corrodes, or eats away, only the metal exposed by the the steel needle. A few minutes is all it takes for the acid to etch the plate.

11. THE PRINTING PROCESS ✦
As the printer turns the wheel on the press, the entire assembly of bed, plate, paper, and felt blanket passes between the machine's two rollers. The great pressure of the rollers forces the damp paper into the etched grooves of the plate to absorb the ink.

✦ 10. THE PRINTING PRESS
The plate is placed on the bed of a printing press, which moves on gears between two rollers. A sheet of damp paper is laid gently on top of the plate and is covered with a felt blanket.

REMBRANDT'S ✦ ETCHINGS
In Europe, the seventeenth century was the "golden age" of making prints, and Rembrandt stands out as one of the finest etchers of all time. He took advantage of all the expressive possibilities the etching process had to offer. Two examples of his work are *Windmill* (top), from 1641, and *Faust* (bottom), from about 1652. Both are kept at the Rijksmuseum in Amsterdam.

✦8. INKING
After all the acid is washed off, the wax is removed from the plate with turpentine, which is a kind of paint thinner or remover. Then, ink is brushed on or rolled over the etched surface of the plate. The inking process is done over a special stove that heats the plate to ensure the ink fills all the etched lines.

✦9. CLEANING
The surface of the plate is carefully wiped with a linen cloth so that ink remains only in the etched grooves.

7. WASHING ✦
The plate is washed in water to remove all traces of acid.

REMBRANDT'S LIFE
When, in 1661, Hendrickje became ill, she made a will, leaving her property to Cornelia and, in case of the child's death, to Titus. The will protected Cornelia's inheritance from the claims of creditors. Hendrickje appointed Rembrandt Cornelia's guardian, however, so he could enjoy her estate during his lifetime. Also that year, Rembrandt painted *The Conspiracy of Claudius Civilis* for Amsterdam's Town Hall. In 1663, however, the picture was removed and returned to Rembrandt. Despite the apparent insult, the public still admired the artist and continued to buy his etchings.

SELF-PORTRAITS

In the 1600s, artists painted many self-portraits, sometimes including symbols of their professions in the pictures. Rembrandt, for example, is holding his palette and brushes in the self-portrait below. The two circles on the wall behind him have been interpreted as everything from symbols of the perfection of God to the circular world maps many people had hanging on their walls in those days.

♦ THE WORK
Self-Portrait with a Palette, c. 1665, oil on canvas, 45 x 37 inches (114 x 94 cm), (Kenwood House, London). This self-portrait was neither signed nor dated. Its age is based on how old Rembrandt looks, especially compared to the self-portraits he produced in his final years, in which he appears more aged. The painting seems unfinished. The turban looks as if it has only been roughed in. The hands are also treated in a sketchy way. If the work had been completed, the significance of the two circles behind the artist might be clear. Restoration work done on the painting fifty years ago revealed some damage to both the canvas and the painting's surface, and X-rays showed that Rembrandt had repainted certain areas.

♦ YOUTHFUL WORK
This self-portrait, c. 1629 (Mauritshuis, The Hague), has the polished look typical of Rembrandt's early work.

♦ A LATE WORK
This self-portrait (Uffizi, Florence) is dated 1662.

♦ SELF-PORTRAIT ETCHINGS
These etchings, one (top) painted in 1630 (Bibliothèque Nationale, Paris), the other (above) in 1629 (Rijksmuseum, Amsterdam), show how Rembrandt also made self-portraits as studies of different facial expressions.

A STUDY OF STYLE

About forty of Rembrandt's self-portraits have survived. Studying them is one way to follow the development of his artistic style. His early self-portraits have the highly polished look typical of the time and include more details than later ones. His mature self-portraits tend to have thick coats of paint and richly worked surfaces. Self-portraits from his final years are so sketchy they are almost Impressionistic.

MIDDLE-AGED ♦
Apparently inspired by the "Old Masters" Raphael and Titian, Rembrandt painted himself in sixteenth-century style in *Self-Portrait at the Age of 34*, 1640 (National Gallery, London), as if to put himself on a par with the great artists of the past.

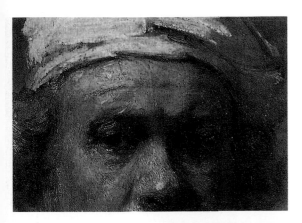

♦COLOR, TEXTURE, AND TECHNIQUE
Rembrandt's technique was distinctive in the way he used paint as a material, not only to indicate the color of a surface but also to convey texture. Although often accused of applying paint in a lumpy way, he was, in fact, constantly experimenting with texture. Some of his later works, as seen in these two details (top left and right) from *Self-Portrait with a Palette*, contain areas where paint is applied very thinly. Although the work is considered unfinished, its technique still serves to illustrate how Rembrandt tried to suggest reality rather than represent it.

SELF-IMPROVEMENT ♦
Art historians have some doubts as to who painted *Self-Portrait as Young Man*, c. 1634 (Uffizi, Florence), and who is actually pictured. X-rays suggest that the painting may be a young Rembrandt, retouched to soften his features and appear less stern.

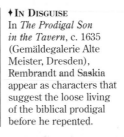

♦IN COSTUME
In many self-portraits, Rembrandt appears in costume. *Self-Portrait in Fancy Dress*, 1634–1636 (Mauritshuis, The Hague), is a good example. Rembrandt and members of his family are also seen costumed in paintings of biblical and mythical subjects, perhaps to avoid paying models.

♦IN DISGUISE
In *The Prodigal Son in the Tavern*, c. 1635 (Gemäldegalerie Alte Meister, Dresden), Rembrandt and Saskia appear as characters that suggest the loose living of the biblical prodigal before he repented.

♦IN ORIENTAL ATTIRE
Self-Portrait in Oriental Attire, c. 1631 (Musèe du Petit Palais, Paris), is one of few paintings in which Rembrandt is standing. The dog is another remarkable, but probably not original, feature.

STILL-LIFE PAINTINGS

Paintings in seventeenth-century Holland were merchandise, or goods to be bought and sold, and artists were businessmen who kept the market well-supplied with their merchandise. When looking for still-life paintings, which represented everyday objects such as a jug or a bowl of fruit, purchasers wanted as realistic a depiction as possible. In painting still lifes, Dutch artists tried to imitate reality to perfection. They reproduced flowers, animals, and ornamental items as if they were competing with a craftsman or with nature itself. Their near-perfect products explain the great success of still-life paintings at this time.

◆ A STILL-LIFE MASTER
Abraham van Beyeren (c. 1620–1690) started out painting fish, but toward the middle of the century he became a master of lavish still lifes. Many of them included fish or other sea creatures, such as the crab in the left foregound of *Sumptuous Still Life*, c. 1655 (Mauritshuis, The Hague).

REMBRANDT'S LIFE
A terrible plague broke out in Amsterdam in 1663, killing about 1,700 people, including Hendrickje. Rembrandt had her buried in a rented tomb in Amsterdam's Westerkerk (West Church), but business was bad and commissions were few and far between, so paying the rent was difficult. Things improved in about 1665, when Titus successfully recovered a debt, and Rembrandt was asked to paint *The Jewish Bride*.

TABLES ◆
Tables covered with fine fabrics, elegant glassware, silver and gold vessels, jugs of wine, and assorted foods were typical in the still-life paintings of Dutch artists.

1. Willem Kalf (1622–1693), *Still Life*, 1659 (Mauritshuis, The Hague)
2. Willem Claesz Heda (1594–1680), *Still Life*, 1634 (Boymans, Rotterdam)
3. Willem Claesz Heda, *Breakfast with a Crab*, 1648 (State Hermitage, St. Petersburg)

ANIMALS ◆
Among Dutch wildlife painters of the seventeenth century, Melchior d' Hondecoeter (1636–1695) has few equals when it comes to painting birds and fowl. Both his father and grandfather also painted animals.

1. Melchior d' Hondecoeter, *Peacocks and Ducks*, c. 1680 (Wallace Collection, London)
2. Carel Fabritius (1622–1654), *The Goldfinch*, 1654 (Mauritshuis, The Hague)

FLOWERS ◆
In the Middle Ages, flowers had been symbols of beauty and rebirth. In Dutch paintings of the 1600s, a flower was just a flower.
1. Maria van Oosterwyck (1630–1693), *Flowers and Fruit*, c. 1670 (Palatine Gallery, Florence)
2. Ambrosius Bosschaert the Elder (1573–1621), *Vase with Flowers in a Window*, c. 1618 (Mauritshuis, The Hague)

2

3

2

2

THREE LEMONS ♦
The pictures to the right are details of the lemons in the three paintings to the left. Careful training and many years of experience went into developing the technical skill needed to produce such realistic detail. Although many still-life paintings were sold in the 1600s, their low cost made earning a living from art alone almost impossible for most Dutch painters. Many of them had to take on other jobs. Willem van de Velde, for example, managed a linen factory, and Jan Steen ran an inn.

1

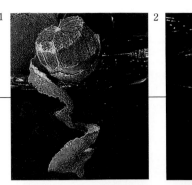

2

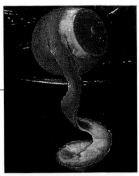

3

REMBRANDT ♦
Still life was not a main genre for Rembrandt. In fact, *Dead Peacocks*, c. 1639 (Rijksmuseum, Amsterdam), may be his only still-life painting.

VANITAS ♦
A special type of still life painting that was popular throughout Europe during the 1600s is known as *Vanitas*. It is a kind of symbolic painting, that features skulls, hourglasses, decayed fruit, and faded flowers as reminders of how quickly life passes and the certainty of death. Aelbert Jansz van der Schoor (c. 1603–1672), *Vanitas Still Life*, c. 1660 (Rijksmuseum, Amsterdam).

THE JEWISH BRIDE

In portrait painting, depicting subjects as biblical
or historical characters was fairly common. In
The Jewish Bride, Rembrandt's subjects appear to
be cast as Isaac and Rebecca from a story in the
Book of Genesis. The true identity of the subjects
is uncertain. Some think they are Rembrandt's
son, Titus, and his wife, Magdalena.

ANOTHER BRIDE ♦
This pen-and-
ink drawing is a pre-
liminary study for
*The Great Jewish
Bride*, c. 1635
(Nationalmuseum,
Stockholm), one of
Rembrandt's
earliest etchings.

♦ TITUS AS A
YOUNG MAN
Rembrandt's son,
Titus, was about
twenty-one years
old when the artist
painted *Portrait
of Titus*, c. 1660
(Louvre, Paris),
shown above.
In this portrayal,
Titus looks much
younger than the
male subject in
The Jewish Bride,
which suggests
that the figures in
the famous portrait
are not Titus and
Magdalena.

BEST VIEWED FROM A DISTANCE

In his later years, Rembrandt's lifelong experiments with paint had led him far from
mid-1600s tastes for highly polished, Baroque-
style paintings. *The Jewish Bride* is characteristic
of Rembrandt's late style, in which he used a
technique known as "impasto." Thick layers
of paint are spread on the canvas and worked
over the surface with a brush or a palette knife.
The thickness of the paint leaves visible brush
strokes or, if a knife is used, scoop marks. To
experience their full effect, paintings made using
the impasto technique are best viewed from
a distance. Unfortunately, few of Rembrandt's
contemporaries appreciated these paintings.

ANOTHER ♦
UNKNOWN WOMAN
The subject in
Rembrandt's paint-
ing *Portrait
of a Well-Dressed
Young Woman*,
c. 1665 (Museum
of Fine Arts,
Montreal), was prob-
ably Titus's wife,
Magdalena
van Loo. Some peo-
ple, however, believe
the woman in the
portrait is
Hendrickje Stoffels.

VENETIAN STYLE ✦
The blended colors and blurred outlines of Rembrandt's final style are similar to the work of Venetian artist Titian (c. 1485–1576), whose *Pietà*, 1570–1576 (Accademia, Venice), is shown.

✦ THE WIDOW AND HER FAMILY
Two of the figures in Rembrandt's *Family Portrait*, c. 1669 (Duke Anton Ulrich Museum, Brunswick), are, most likely, Magdalena and her daughter, Titia, who was born after Titus died.

✦ COLORS AND TEXTURE
Painting *The Jewish Bride*, Rembrandt used variations of only two basic colors. The groom's garments are shades of green-gold, with full, rich color in the foreground sleeve and moderate to dull tones in less prominent areas. The bride's dress is shades of red-orange, splashed with glimmering highlights through the bodice, which is the part of the dress from the waist up. Rembrandt applied the paint in lumps and flakes to suggest the texture of the fabrics. He successfully used similar methods of paint application in other works to make objects of all kinds stand out and look real. Because of his technique, Rembrandt's works have to be viewed from a distance. Even he warned his customers not to step too close, saying, "You would find the smell of the paint offensive." Disapproving of the technique, Dutch history painter Gérard de Lairesse is reported to have said that the paint "runs all over the picture to form a dirty mess."

REMBRANDT'S STUDENTS

Rembrandt's workshop was no different from any other school run by a well-known artist. The young men who came to study with Rembrandt wanted to paint like he did and increase their chances of having financially successful careers as artists. Most of Rembrandt's students had already completed an initial apprenticeship with another teacher before coming to Rembrandt for additional study and training. The rules of the painters' guild specified that works produced by students during their time in a workshop would be signed by the master and marketed as his work. Only after a student's training in the workshop had ended could that student think of benefitting financially from his own talent or setting up a workshop of his own.

♦ **THE MASTER AND HIS STUDENTS AT WORK**
This engraving of Rembrandt's workshop shows the master with his students, practicing life drawing.

REMBRANDT'S LIFE

In 1668, Titus married Magdalena van Loo, but he died only a few months later. In March 1669, Magdelena gave birth to their daughter, Titia. In September of that year, Rembrandt painted *Simeon with the Infant Jesus*. It was probably his last work because he died on October 4, 1669. Like Hendrickje, he was buried in a rented tomb in Amsterdam's Westerkerk, although the exact location of the tomb is not known. Rembrandt was alone during the last months of his life. Most of society had never completely accepted his attitudes, and his paintings no longer suited the tastes of the general public. After his death, Rembrandt van Rijn was forgotten even by critics.

♦ **GERRIT DOU**
(1613–1675)
A member of the workshop from 1628 to 1631, Gerrit Dou was Rembrandt's first student. He was a patient artist with great attention to detail, who, as a successful genre painter, stayed true to the master's early, highly polished style (*The Charlatan*, 1652, Boymans, Rotterdam).

♦ **SAMUEL VAN HOOGSTRATEN**
(1627–1678)
Van Hoogstraten joined the workshop in 1640. Only his early works, however, show that he was Rembrandt's student. He became a genre painter, etcher, poet, and art theorist, but his specialty was perspective effects (*Self-Portrait*, 1645, Prince of Liechtenstein Collection, Vaduz).

♦ **GOVAERT FLINCK**
(1615–1660)
As a student of Rembrandt from about 1633 to 1636, Flinck developed a very similar style. Later, he adopted a polished, classical style and became a well-known portrait painter. He was also awarded a number public commissions (*Portrait of Rembrandt*, c. 1633, Gemäldegalerie, Berlin).

♦ **ISAAK DE JOUDERVILLE**
(c. 1612–1648)
First apprenticed in 1629, Jouderville, like Gerrit Dou, was among Rembrandt's earliest students. In 1631, he followed the master to Amsterdam and stayed for about a year, presumably to help Rembrandt with portrait commissions. Jouderville's own portraits clearly imitate Rembrandt's (*Bust of Young Man*, c. 1645, National Gallery of Ireland, Dublin).

✦ GERBRAND VAN DEN EECKHOUT (1621–1674)
In Rembrandt's workshop from 1635 to 1640, Gerbrand developed a love of history painting. Most of his works reflect his master's later style. (*Prophet Eliseus and the Woman of Sunem*, 1664, Museum of Fine Arts, Budapest).

✦ JAN VICTORS (c. 1619–1676)
A strict Calvinist, Victors painted mainly religious works, but he was never a successful artist. Eventually, he quit painting to help nurse plague victims. He died in the Far East, working for the East India Company (*Joseph Recounting His Dreams*, 1651, Kunstmuseum, Düsseldorf).

✦ CAREL FABRITIUS (1622–1654)
Although he died at a relatively young age, leaving only about a dozen known works, Fabritius is considered by some to be Rembrandt's most gifted student. His distinctly original style can also be seen in the works of Jan Vermeer (*Portrait of Abraham de Potter*, c. 1648, Rijksmuseum, Amsterdam).

✦ FERDINAND BOL (1616–1680)
Bol studied with two other masters before joining Rembrandt's workshop, in about 1636. Then, in 1642, he started his own workshop, specializing in Baroque-style portraits and history and religious paintings (*Elisha Refuses Naaman's Gifts*, 1661, Historisch Museum, Amsterdam).

✦ WILLEM DROST (1633–1659)
Not much is known about Drost's life, but it appears that he studied with Rembrandt in about 1650 and, recently, has been given credit for a number of works originally believed to be Rembrandt's. Drost also painted with Jan Vermeer (*The Vision of Daniel*, c. 1650, Gemäldegalerie, Berlin).

✦ NICOLAES MAES (1634–1693)
Maes studied with Rembrandt for about six years, from 1648 to 1654. His early works were genre paintings, which were distinguished by their Rembrandt-style use of color. In the 1660s, however, he started painting portraits and his style became more like Van Dyck's or Rubens' (*Portrait of Jacob Trip*, c. 1660, Museum of Fine Arts, Budapest).

✦ BARENT FABRITIUS (1624–1673)
Barent was the younger brother of Carel Fabritius, who may have been his teacher. Whether Barent also studied with Rembrandt is uncertain, but his paintings, which are mainly portraits and history paintings, have the look of the Rembrandt school (*Peter in the House of Cornelius*, detail, 1653, Duke Anton Ulrich Museum, Brunswick).

♦ TIME LINE

1606	Rembrandt Harmenszoon van Rijn is born on July 15 in Leiden, Holland. His father owns a successful mill on the Rhine River.
1609	Having declared independence from Spanish rule in 1579, the seven northern United Provinces sign a truce with Spain.
1621	Rembrandt becomes a student of Jacob van Swanenburgh, a local painter who has a workshop in Leiden.
1624	To continue his studies with a more talented master, Rembrandt goes to Amsterdam and joins the workshop of Pieter Lastman. After six months, he returns to Leiden and opens a workshop in partnership with Jan Lievens.
1625	Prince Frederick Henry of Orange is named stadholder (governor) of the United Provinces.
1626	The Dutch West India Company buys a North American peninsula called Mannahatta from the Algonquin Indians and founds Nieuw Amsterdam, later renamed New York.
1628	Fifteen-year-old Gerrit Dou joins Rembrandt and Lievens as their first student, indicating their workshop's growing importance.
1630	Rembrandt and Lievens gain the attention of Constantijn Huygens at The Hague.
1631	Rembrandt moves to Amsterdam. Joining the household of art dealer Hendrick van Uylenburgh, he meets and falls in love with Hendrick's wealthy niece, Saskia.
1632	Rembrandt paints *The Anatomy Lesson of Dr. Nicolaes Tulp*, his first important commission in Amsterdam. Baruch Spinoza is born in Amsterdam.
1634	Rembrandt marries Saskia, gaining her wealth and social standing. Prince Frederick Henry commissions Rembrandt to do a series of paintings of Christ's Passion.
1639	Rembrandt and Saskia move to a large house on St. Anthoniesbreestraat, where Rembrandt expands his impressive art collection.
1642	Saskia dies. Rembrandt hires Geertje Dircz to help him raise his infant son, Titus, born June 14, 1641. Dircz, a widow, becomes Rembrandt's mistress.
1648	Philip IV of Spain signs a peace treaty with the United Provinces, ending more than seventy years of conflict.
1651	The United Provinces go to war with Britain after Oliver Cromwell passes the Navigation Act, establishing a British monopoly on colonial trade and closing its empire to foreign ships.
1656	The war with Britain intensifies Rembrandt's shaky financial situation because creditors are no longer able to carry his huge debts. Dutch authorities inventory his possessions, and his art collection is sold off at three public auctions in 1657 and 1658.
1663	The plague breaks out in Amsterdam. One of its victims is Hendrickje Stoffels, Rembrandt's companion since 1648 and the mother of Rembrandt's daughter, Cornelia.
1667	Cosimo III de' Medici, the Grand Duke of Tuscany, Italy, comes to Amsterdam on business. Wanting to see the famous artist's work, he visits Rembrandt's workshop.
1669	Rembrandt dies on October 4. He is buried in a rented tomb in Amsterdam's Westerkerk.

♦ GLOSSARY

allegory: a story or painting that uses symbolic characters or actions to make a statement about the human condition

aristocrats: nobles and other people of the wealthy and privileged upper classes

capital: the money, equipment, and materials available to start and support a business

censorship: the process of doing away with activities and materials judged as harmful for moral or religious reasons

clergy: religious people, formally authorized to serve a church and its members

contemporaries: individuals who live in the same time period

heretics: people who dispute or act against the laws and teachings of a religion

patrons: people who use their wealth and social standing to support and protect valued individuals and causes

planisphere: a special map that represents the circles of a sphere on a flat surface

refugees: people who go to another country or region to escape danger or persecution

still life: a drawing or painting in which the subject is a group of inanimate objects

virginal: a small pianolike instrument, similar to a harpsichord

WEB SITES

The Many Faces of Rembrandt van Rijn
*dir.yahoo.com/thespark/749/
the-many-faces-of-rembrandt-van-rijn*
Follow links to a chronology of Rembrandt's self-portraits and related information.

Rembrandt
cgfa.dotsrc.org/rembrand/
Includes a biography and pages of thumbnails linked to full-page views of the artist's works.

Rembrandthuis (Rembrandt House)
www.rembrandthuis.nl/cms_pages/
Tour Rembrandt's house in Amsterdam, now a museum dedicated to his life and his art.

♦ LIST OF WORKS INCLUDED

(Works reproduced in their entirety are indicated with the letter E; those of which only a detail is featured are followed by the letter D.)

The works reproduced in this book are listed here, with their date (when known), the place they are currently housed, and the page number. The numbers in bold type refer to the credits on 64. Abbreviations: BMR, Boymans-van Beuningen Museum, Rotterdam; HMA, Historisch Museum, Amsterdam; KMV Kunsthistorisches Museum, Vienna; RA, Rijksmuseum, Amsterdam.

ANONYMOUS
1 *The Anatomy Theatre at Leiden University,* 1664, engraving from *Atlas* by Frederick Müller (Bibliothèque Nationale, Paris) 35 E; **2** *Anna and Tobit,* engraving of a work by Marten van Heemskerck (Rijksprentenkabinett, Amsterdam) 21 E; **3** *Map of Manhattan,* 1664 (British Library, London) 39 E; **4** *The Netherlands in the Form of a Lion,* print often attributed to Jodocus Hondius, c.1611 (University Library, Amsterdam); **5** *The Synod of Dort* (Historisch Museum, Rotterdam) 28 E; **6** *William III of Orange and His Predecessors,* engraving, 1672 (Historisch Museum, Rotterdam) 28 E
AVERCAMP, HENDRICK
7 *Winter Scene,* c.1608 (RA) 33 D
BERCKHEYDE, JOB ADRIAENSZ
8 *The Amsterdam Stock Exchange,* c. 1668 (BMR) 14 D
BEYEREN, ABRAHAM VAN
9 *Still Life with Crab and Fruit* (Mauritshuis, The Hague) 56 E
BOL, FERDINAND
10 *Allegory of the Admiralty,* c.1660 (HMA) 18 D; **11** *The Courage of Fabricius in the Camp of Pyrrhus,* 1650 (HMA) 19 E; **12** *Elisha Refusing Naaman's Gifts,* 1661 (HMA) 61 E; **13** *The Officers of the Wine Merchants' Guild,* c.1640-50 (Alte Pinakothek, Munich) 25 E; **14** *Portrait of Elisabeth Bas* (attr.) c.1640 (RA) 25 E; **15** *The Regents of the Leprosarium* (HMA) 29 E
BOSCH, HIERONYMOUS
16 *Hermits' Triptych,* 1510 (Doge's Palace, Venice) 7 D
BOSSCHAERT THE ELDER, PIETER
17 *Vase of Flowers,* c.1620 (Mauritshuis, The Hague) 57 E
BRUEGEL THE ELDER, PIETER
18 *Huntsmen in the Snow,* 1565 (KMV) 7 D
CANALETTO, BYNAME OF ANTONIO CANAL
19 *The Campo Santi Apostoli,* 1731-35 (private collection) 30 E
CATS, JACOB
20 *The Night Watch,* copied from Remberandt's work, 1779 (RA) 51 E
DOU, GERRIT
21 *Anna and Tobit in his Blindness,* c.1630 (National Gallery, London) 21 E; **22** *The Charlatan,* 1652 (BMR) 60 E
DROST, WILLEM
23 *Daniel's Vision,* 1650-52 (Gemäldegalerie, Berlin) 61 E and D
DÜRER, ALBRECHT
24 *Portrait of Willibald Pirkheimer,* woodcut, 1524-52 E
DYCK, ANTHONY VAN
25 *Portrait of a Man and his Son,* 1628-29 (Louvre, Paris) 27 E and D
EECKHOUT, GERBRAND VAN DEN
26 *Christ in the Synagogue at Nazareth,* 1658 (National Gallery of Ireland, Dublin) 19 E; **27** *The Prophet Elisha and the Shunammite Woman,* 1664 (Szépmüveszeti Museum, Budapest) 61 D
EVERDINGEN, CAESAR VAN
28 *The Glorification of the Burgonmasters of Amsterdam* (Kunsthalle, Hamburg) 18 E
EYCK, JAN VAN
29 *Giovanni Arnólfini and his Wife,* 1434 (National Gallery, London) 6 E and D, 7 D
FABRITIUS, BARENT
30 *Peter in the House of Cornelius,* 1635 (Duke Anton Ulrich Museum, Brunswick) 61 E
FABRITIUS, CAREL
31 *The Goldfinch,* 1654 (Mauritshuis, The Hague) 57 E; **32** *Portrait of Abraham de Potter,* c.1648 (RA) 61 E
FLEURY, JOSEPH-NICOLAS ROBERT-
33 *Galileo before the Holy Office,* 1847 (Louvre, Paris) 29 D
FLINCK, GOVAERT
34 *Portrait of Rembrandt,* c.1633 (Gemäldegalerie, Berlin) 60 E; **35** *Portrait of Rembrandt,* 1636 (RA) 24 D
HALS, FRANS
36 *Banquet of the Officers of the Militia Company of St George,* 1616 (Frans Halsmuseum, Haarlem); **37** *Couple Out of Doors,* 1621 (RA) 24 E; **38** *Hille Bobbe,* 1630 (Musée des Beaux-Arts, Lille) 25 E; **39** *The Merry Topper,* 1657 (RA) 25 E; **40** *Portrait of Nicolaes Hasselaer,* c.1635 (RA) 24 D
HEDA, WILLEM CLAESZ
41 *Luncheon with Lobsters,* 1648 (Hermitage, St Petersburg) 57 E and D; **42** *Still Life,* 1634 (BMR) 57 E and D

HEYDEN, JAN VAN DER
43 *Blazing House,* from the Brandspuitenboeck (HMA) 44 E; **44** *View of the Town Hall* (Louvre, Paris) 32 D
HONDECOETER, MELCHIOR
45 *Peacocks and Ducks,* 1680 (Wallace Collection, London) 56 E
HOOGH, PIETER DE
46 *Courtyard of a House in Delft,* 1658 (Noortman Gallery, London) 45 E; **47** *The Linen Cupboard,* 1658 (RA) 44 E
HOOGSTRATEN, SAMUEL VAN
48 *Interior of a Dutch House,* magic box, 1650 (National Gallery, London) 31 E; **49** *Self-portrait,* 1645 (Prince of Lichtenstein Collection, Vaduz) 60 E
JOUDERVILLE, ISAAC
50 *Bust of a Young Man,* c.1631 (National Gallery of Ireland, Dublin) 60 E
KALFF, WILLEM
51 *Still Life,* c.1650 (Mauritshuis, The Hague) 56 E, 57 D
KEYSER, THOMAS DE
52 *The Anatomy Lesson of Doctor Egbertsz* (HMA) 35 E
LAIRESSE, GÉRARD DE
53 *The Peoples of the World Paying Homage to Amsterdam,* c.1670-80 (HMA) 18 D, 19 E
LASTMAN, PIETER
54 *Deposition,* c.1620 (Musée des Beaux-Arts, Lille) 18 E; **55** *Susanna and the Elders,* 1614 (Gemäldegalerie, Berlin) 19 D
LIEVENS, JAN
56 *Pilate Washing His Hands,* 1625-30 (Lakenhal, Leiden) 18 E
LYON, JACOB
57 *Captain Hoogkame's Company* (HMA) 25 D
MAES, NICOLAES
58 *Portrait of Jacob Trip,* 1659-60 (Mauritshuis, The Hague) 61 E
MANTEGNA, ANDREA
59 *Dead Christ,* before 1506 (Brera, Milan) 35 E
MEMLING, HANS
60 *St John the Evangelist Altarpiece,* 1479 (Memling Museum, Bruges) 6 E, 7 D
MICKER, JAN CHRISTIAENSZ
61 *View of Amsterdam* (HMA) 32 E
MIEREVELD, PIETER VAN
62 *The Anatomy Lesson of Doctor van der Meer* (Gemeente Museum, Delft) 35 E
MIERIS, FRANS VAN
63 *Portrait of Woman with Parrot,* (National Gallery, London) 25 E; **64** *Two Old People at Table,* 1655-60 (Uffizi, Florence) 45 E
MOSTAERT, GILLIS
65 *The Sack of a Village,* late sixteenth century (KMV) 9 E
OSTADE, ADRIAEN VAN
66 *Peasant Gathering,* 1661 (RA) 45 D
OSTERWELT, MARIA VAN
67 *Flowers, Fruit, Insects* (Palatine Gallery, Florence) 56 E
PAX, H.A.
68 *The Princes of Orange in the Buitenhof at The Hague* (Mauritshuis, The Hague) 24 D
PETRUS CHRISTUS
69 *Portrait of a Young Girl,* c.1445 (Staatliche Museen, Berlin) 9 E
POTTER, PAULUS
70 *The Bull,* 1647 (Mauritshuis, The Hague) 33 E
REMBRANDT
71 *The Anatomy Lesson of Doctor Deyman,* 1656 (HMA) 35 E; **72** preliminary sketch for *The Anatomy Lesson of Doctor Deyman* (HMA) 34 E; **73** *The Anatomy Lesson of Doctor Tulp,* 1632 (Mauritshuis, The Hague) 34 E and D, 35 D; **74** *Anna and Tobit,* 1626 (RA) 20 E and D, 21 D; **75** *Balaam's Ass,* 1626 (Cognaq-Jay Museum, Paris) 19 E; **76** *Child and Dead Peacocks,* c.1639 (RA) 57 E; **77** *Family Portrait,* 1668-69 (Duke Anton Ulrich Museum, Brunswick) 59 E; **78** *Faust,* engraving, 1652 53 E; **79** *The Jewish Bride,* 1668 58 E, 59 D; **80** *Landscape with Bridge,* c.1640 (RA) 33 E; **81** *The Night Watch,* 1642 (RA) 50 E and D, 51 D; **82** *The Painter's Studio,* c.1648 (Louvre, Paris) 48 E; **83** *Portrait of Couple in an Interior,* 1633 (Isabella Stewart Gardner Museum, Boston) 27 E; **84** *Portrait of Hendrickje,* c.1654 (Louvre, Paris) 46 E; **85** *Portrait of Jacob de Gheyn III,* 1632 (Dulwich Art Gallery, London) 21 D, 26 E and D; **86** *Portrait of Maria Trip,* c.1639 (RA) 26 E; **87** *Portrait of Maurits Huygens,* 1632 (Hamburger Kunsthalle, Hamburg) 26 D, 27 E and E; **88** *Portrait of Philip Lucasz,* 1635 (National Gallery, London) 37 E; **89** *Portrait of Seated Man,* c.1632 (KMV) 27 E; **90** *Portrait of Seated Woman,* c.1632 (KMV) 27 E; **91** *Portrait of Titus,* c.1660 (Louvre, Paris) 58 E; **92** *Portrait of Well-dressed Young Man,* c.1665 (Montreal Museum of Fine Arts,

Montreal) 58 E; **93** *Rembrandt's Father,* c.1630-31 (Mauritshuis, The Hague) 46 E; **94** *Rembrandt's Mother with her Hand on her Chest,* engraving, 1631 (Bibliothèque Nationale, Paris) 20 E; **96** *Saskia,* drawing, c.1640 (Musée Bonnat, Bayonne) 46 E; **97** *Saskia in Arcadian Costume,* 1635 (National Gallery, London) 46 E; **98** *Self-portrait,* c.1628 (RA) 54 E; **99** *Self-portrait,* 1629 (RA) 54 E; **100** *Self-portrait,* c.1629 (Mauritshuis, The Hague) 54 E; **101** *Self-portrait,* 1630 (Bibliothèque Nationale, Paris) 54 E; **102** *Self-portrait,* c.1662 (Uffizi, Florence) 54 E; **103** *Self-portrait,* c.1665 (Kenwood House, London) 54 E; **104** *Self-portrait at the Age of 34,* 1640 (National Gallery, London) 54 E; **105** *Self-portrait in Fancy Clothing,* 1635-36 (Mauritshuis, The Hague) 55 E; **106** *Self-portrait* or *The Prodigal Son in the Tavern,* c.1635 (Gemäldegalerie, Dresden) 55 E; **107** *Study for the Jewish Bride,* pen drawing, c.1635 (Nasional Museet, Stockholm) 58 E; **108** *Study of a Head,* ink drawing, c.1636 (Barber Institute, Birmingham) 20 D; **109** *Titus as a Monk,* 1660 (RA) 47 D; **110** *Tobit Accusing Anna of Stealing the Kid,* 1645 (Gemäldegalerie, Berlin) 21 E; **111** *View of Amsterdam* (RA) 33 E; **112** *Windmill,* engraving, 1641 (RA) 53 E
REMBRANDT (ATTRIB.)
113 *Self-portrait,* 1639-40 (Uffizi, Florence) 55 E; **114** *Self-portrait* or *Portrait of Rembrandt in Oriental Costume with Poodle,* c.1631 (Petit Palais, Paris) 55 E
REMBRANDT (WORKSHOP)
115 *Master and Pupils Drawing from Life,* engraving (Landesmuseum, Darmstadt) 60 E
RUBENS, PETER PAUL
116 *The Miracles of St Ignatius Loyola,* 1618-19 (KMV) 9 E; **117** *Portrait of Albert of Austria,* 1613-15 (KMV) 8 E; **118** *Portrait of Isabella of Habsburg,* 1613-15 (KMV) 8 E; **119** *Self-portrait with his Wife Isabella,* 1609-10 (Alte Pinakothek, Munich) 8 E; **120** *Self-portrait,* c.1649 (KMV) 9 E
RUYSDAEL, JACOB VAN
121 *View of Haarlem* (Gemäldegalerie, Berlin) 33 E
RUYSDAEL, SALOMON
122 *Landscape with River,* 1649 (RA) 33 E
SAENREDAM, PIETER
123 *Church of St Adolf at Assenfeld,* 1649 (RA) 9 E; **124** *Interior of St Bavo's, Haarlem,* 1635 (RA) 45 E; **125** *Interior of St Lawrence Church, Alkmaar,* 1661 (BMR) 44 E
SCHOOR, AELBERT JANSZ VAN DER
126 *Vanitas* (RA) 57 E
STEEN, JAN
127 *The Cabaret,* 1660-70 (Mauritshuis, The Hague) 44 D; **128** *The Prince's Birthday,* 1660-70 (HMA) 45 E
SWANEVELT, HERMAN VAN
129 *Landscape with Figures,* c.1640 (Uffizi, Florence) 32 D
TER BORCH, GERARD
130 *Self-portrait,* c.1670 (Mauritshuis, The Hague) 25 E
TITIAN
131 Study for *Martyrdom of St Peter* (Louvre, Paris) 47 E; **132** *Pietà,* 1570-76 (Accademia Gallery, Venice) 59 E
VALCKERT, WERNER VAN DE
133 *Distribution of Bread at the Almoezeniershuis,* 1627 (HMA) 29 E
VELDE, JAN VAN DE
134 *Anna and Tobit,* engraving from a drawing done by Buytewech in 1629 (Rijksprentenkabinett, Amsterdam) 21 E
VELDE, WILLEM VAN DE
135 *The Port of Amsterdam,* 1686 (HMA) 33 D
VERMEER, JAN
136 *The Artist's Studio,* c.1665 (KMV) 38 D, 40 E and D; **137** *The Astronomer,* c.1668 (Louvre, Paris) 38 D, 41 E; **138** *The Geographer,* c.1668 (Städelsches Kunstinstitut, Frankfurt) 39 E and 40 D; **139** *The Glass of Wine,* 1660-61 (Gemäldegalerie, Berlin) 41 E; **140** *Lady at the Virginals,* c.1670 (National Gallery, London) 41 D; **141** *The Music Lesson,* c.1664 (Buckingham Palace, London) 31 E; **142** *Woman with a Pearl Necklace,* 1662-65 (Gemäldegalerie, Berlin) 41 E; **143** *Woman Reading a Letter,* 1662-65 (RA) 41 E; **144** *View of Delft,* 1661 (Mauritshuis, The Hague) 41 E
VICTORS, JAN
145 *Joseph Recounting his Dreams,* 1651 (Kunstmuseum, Düsseldorf) 61 E
VISSCHER, CLAES
146 *View of the Port of Amsterdam,* engraving, 1630 (private collection) 11 D
VROOM, HENDRICK
147 *The Port of Amsterdam* (Schlessheim Castle, Bavaria) 32 D
WITTE, EMANUEL DE
148 *Church Interior,* 1617-22 (Musée Jeanne d'Aboville, La Fere) 45 E
WOUWERMAN, PHILIPS
149 *Battle Scene,* 1650 (National Gallery, London) 19 E

◆ INDEX

A

Albert of Austria, archduke 8, 9
Amsterdam 11, 22-23, 34, 37, 38 42,
- Amstel River 15, 22, 23
- Bank of Amsterdam 14
- guilds 14, 15
- musketeers 50-51
- Nieuwe Kerk 14, 23
- origins 23
- stock exchange 14, 23
- town hall 14, 23
anatomy theaters 34, 35
Anna and Tobit 20-21
Avercamp, Hendrick 33

B

Banning Cocq, Frans 5, 50
Berckheyde, Job Adriaensz 14
Beyeren, Abraham van 56
Blaeu, Willem Jansz 16, 17
Bol, Ferdinand 18, 24, 29, 61
Bolnes, Catharina 40, 41
booksellers 16, 17
Bosch, Hieronymus 7
Bosschaert the Elder, Ambrosius 56
Braun, Georg 38
Bruegel the Elder, Pieter 7
Buytewech, Willem 21

C

Calvinism 24, 44
camera obscura 30, 31
Canaletto (Giovanni Antonio Canal) 30
cartography 8, 16, 17, 32, 38-39
censorship 16
Christus, Petrus 6

D

Descartes, René 16, 22
Dircx, Geertje 42, 62
Dort, Synod of 28
Dou, Gerrit 21, 22, 60
Dreyer, Carl Theodor 35
Drost, Willem 61
Dürer, Albrecht 52

Dutch East India Company 16, 17, 36, 37, 39
Dyck, Anthony van 9, 24, 27

E

Eeckhout, Gerbrand van den 18-19, 61
Elzevier, Louis 16
engraving 52
etching 52-53
Everdingen, Caesar van 18
Eyck, Jan van 6, 47

F

Fabritius, Barent 61
Fabritius, Carel 61
Flemish art 6-7 24
Fleury, Joseph-Nicolas Robert-29
Flinck, Govaert 24, 60
fluyt 36
Frederick Henry, Prince of Orange 5, 28
Friedländer, Max 44

G

Galileo Galilei 16, 28, 29
genre painting 44-45
Gheyn III, Jacob de 26, 27
guilds 14, 15

H

Haarlem school 24
Hals, Frans 5, 24, 25
Heda, Willem Claesz 56
Heyden, Jan van der 32, 44
history painting 18-19
Hogenberg, Frans 38
Holland
- architecture 42-43
- Calvinist 24
- canals 10, 11, 42
- dikes 22
- Golden Age 4, 16
- homes 42-43
- polders 22
- shipbuilding 11, 36
- States General 14, 28
- tolerance 28-29
- trading nation 10-11, 36-37
- United Provinces 8, 10, 28

see also Amsterdam
Hondecoeter, Melchior d' 56
Hondius, Jodocus 8, 17, 38
Hoogstraten, Samuel van 31, 51, 60
Huygens, Constantijn 4, 22, 26, 28
Huygens, Maurits 26, 27

I

Inquisition 8, 9
interiors 44-45
Isabella of Spain 8

J

Jouderville, Isack de 60

K

Kalff, Willem 56
Kepler, Johannes 30
Keyser, Thomas de 35

L

Lairesse, Gérard de 18, 59
landscape painting 32-33
Lastman, Pieter 18
Leeuwenhoek, Antony van 28
Leiden 12-13, 16, 17, 18, 35
Lievens, Jan 4, 18, 22
Loo, Magdalena van 58, 59, 60
Lyon, Jacob 24

M

Maes, Nicolaes 61
Manhattan 39
maps, see cartography
Memling, Hans 6, 7
Micker, Jan Christiaensz 32
microscope 28, 30
middle classes 14-15, 18, 24, 32, 44
Mierevelt, Pieter van 35
Mieris, Frans van 24-25, 44-45
Moluccas 39
Mostaert, Gillis 9
Müller, Frederick 35

N

Netherlands, Spanish 8-9, 16

O

optics 30
Oosterwyck, Maria van 56
Orange, House of 28
Ostade, Adriaen van 44-45

P

Pax, H.A. 24
portraiture painting 24-25, 26-27
Potter, Paulus 32-33
printers 17

R

religious paintings 18, 19
Rembrandt
- etchings 53
- film directors 35
- landscapes 32-33
- parents 4, 13, 17, 22, 46
- portraiture 26-27, 34, 37, 46, 47, 50, 51, 58, 59
Rijn, Harmen Gerritsz van (father) 4, 13, 46
Rijn, family van 13, 17
Rubens, Pieter Paul 5, 8, 9
Ruysdael, Jacob van 32
Ruysdael, Salomon 32
Ryther, Augustine 38

S

Saenredam, Pieter 9, 44
Saskia, see Uylenburgh, Saskia van
Schoor, Aelbert Jansz van der 57
Spain, Spanish rule of Netherlands 8
Spinoza, Baruch 5, 28, 29
Stadholders 28
Steen, Jan 44, 57
still life 56-57
Steen, Jan 44, 57
Stoffels, Hendrickje 4, 42, 46, 48, 53, 56, 58
Stuyvesant, Pieter 39
Swanenburgh, Jacob van 18
Swanevelt, Herman van 32

T

Ter Borch, Gerard 24
theodolite 38
Titian, Tiziano Vecellio 47, 59
Titus (son) 4, 42, 46, 47, 48, 53, 58, 60
tulip mania 14, 15
Tulp, Nicolaes Pietersz 5, 34, 35

U

United Provinces, see Holland
Uylenburgh, Hendrick van 4, 22, 28
Uylenburgh, Saskia van 4, 28, 32, 42, 46, 55

V

Valckert, Werner van den 29
Vanitas 57
Velde, Jan van de 21
Velde, Willem van de 32, 57
Vermeer, Jan 5, 28, 30, 31, 38, 39, 40-41, 61
Victors, Jan 61
Visshaert, Claes 11
Vroom, Hendrick 32

W

windmills 12-13, 22
witch hunts 29
Witte, Emanuel de 44
woodcut 52
Wouwerman, Philips 18

Z

Zuytbroeck, Neeldgen (Cornelia) Willemsdr van (mother) 4, 13, 46

◆ CREDITS

(Abbreviations: b, bottom; c, center; l, left; r, right; t, top)
The original and previously unpublished illustrations in this book may be reproduced only with the prior permission of Donati Giudici Associati, who hold the copyright.
The illustrations are by: SERGIO (4/5; 10/11; 12-13; 15 a; 15 b; 29 c; 30/31; 42-43; 46-47; 48-49; 52-53); PAOLA HOLGUIN (11 b; 12 a; 13 a; 15 c; 27 b; 29 a; 30 cs; 43 ac; 43 ad; 43 cd; 52 as); SEBASTIANO RANCHETTI (8 a; 9 a; 10 a; 22-23 a; 28 b); ANDREA RICCIARDI (14-15); THOMAS TROJER (36-37)
ALINARI/BRIDGEMAN/GIRAUDON: 47; ALINARI/GIRAUDON: 27, 41, 43, 62, 83, 109, 124; ALINARI/LAUROS/GIRAUDON: 86, 98, 148; L'AJA, MAURITSHUIS: 33, 51, 58, 68, 75, 128, 130; AMBURGO, HAMBURGER KUNSTHAUS: 30; AMSTERDAMS HISTORISCH MUSEUM: 10, 12, 13, 14, 44, 52, 53, 57, 61, 88, 107, 133, 134; AMSTERDAM, RIJKSMUSEUM: 1, 7, 15,

20, 34, 37, 38, 40, 42, 46, 66, 71, 73, 74, 84, 85, 87, 90, 91, 93, 100, 105, 108, 114, 122, 123, 125, 126, 127, 135; AMSTERDAM, UNIVERSITY LIBRARY: 4; ARTEPHOT: 72, 76, 96; ARTEPHOT/ARTOTEQUE: 11; ARTEPHOT/A.HELD: 101; ARTEPHOT/G.REINOLD: 82; ARTEPHOT/NIMATALLAH: 59; ARCHIVIO GIUNTI, FIRENZE: 19, 29, 48; ARCHIVIO SCALA, FIRENZE: 9, 21, 132, 137; BERLINO, STAATLICHE MUSEEN-PREUBISCHER KULTURBESITZ/JÖRG P. ANDERS: 25, 36, 55, 69, 113, 121, 138, 140; BOSTON, ISABELLA GARDNER-STEWART MUSEUM: 94; BRAUNSCHWEIG, HERZOG ANTON ULRICHMUSEUM: 32; BRIDGEMAN ART LIBRARY: 45, 70, 79, 80, 81, 92, 99, 110, 139, 141, 149; BRIDGEMAN/GIRAUDON 54; DARMSTADT, HESSISCHES LANDESMUSEUM: 115; DR: 146; DUBLINO, NATIONAL GALLERY OF IRELAND: 28, 50; DÜSSELDORF, KUNSTMUSEUM IM EHRENHOF: 145; ERICH LESSING, VIENNA: 16, 18, 31, 39, 60, 65, 89, 95, 103, 104, 106, 116, 117, 118, 119, 120, 136, 144; LEIDA, LAKENHALL: 56; LONDRA, NATIONAL GALLERY:

23, 49, 64, 102; LONDRA, THE ROYAL COLLECTION, HER MAJESTY ELIZABETH II: 143; MONTREAL, MUSEUM OF FINE ARTS: 97; RMN: 35, 131; PARIGI, BIBLIOTHEQUE NATIONALE: 6; ROTTERDAM, ATLAS VAN STOLK: 2, 5; ROGER-VIOLLET: 26, 111; ROTTERDAM, MUSEUM BOYMANS-VAN BEUNINGEN/TOM HAARTSEN: 8, 22, 24; SERGE DOMINGE/MARCO RABATTI: 63, 67, 77, 78, 129; STOCCOLMA, NATJONALMUSEET: 112; VENEZIA, PALAZZO DUCALE: 17
Documenti: Archivio Dogi (p. 35 ad; p. 38 cd; p. 38 cs; p. 39 ad; p. 39 bd); Firenze, Museo della scienza (p. 38 b; p. 39 a); Alinari/Giraudon (p. 16 bs; p. 16 bd); Roger-Viollet: (p. 21 cd, p. 42 a)
DoGi s.r.l. have made every effort to trace other possible copyright holders. If any omissions have been made, they will be corrected at reprint.